## About the Author

Ghaith Hammour is a Syrian writer and journalist, born in Damascus in 1982. He has BA in Mass Communication from Damascus University in Syria, and an MA in Television and Film from Bahcesehir in Turkey. He has articles in several Syrian and Arab media institutions, most notably the London-based newspaper, *Al-Hayat,* the Samir Kassir website, and others. He held the position of editor-in-chief for several websites. He has six publications: *Abyad Qan* 2022—Novel, *Cultural Hegemony Under Totalitarian Regimes* 2023—Study, *Corrupt Empire* 2023—Novel, *Crow and Idols* 2024—Novel, *The President Is A Partner* 2024—Stories.

# In the Shadow of a White Dress

# Ghaith Hammour

Translation by: Nora Hinnawi

# In the Shadow of a White Dress

Olympia Publishers
*London*

www.olympiapublishers.com
OLYMPIA PAPERBACK EDITION

Copyright © Ghaith Hammour 2025

The right of Ghaith Hammour to be identified as author of this work has been asserted in accordance with sections 77 and 78 of the Copyright, Designs and Patents Act 1988.

**All Rights Reserved**

No reproduction, copy or transmission of this publication may be made without written permission.
No paragraph of this publication may be reproduced, copied or transmitted save with the written permission of the publisher, or in accordance with the provisions of the Copyright Act 1956 (as amended).

Any person who commits any unauthorised act in relation to this publication may be liable to criminal prosecution and civil claims for damage.

A CIP catalogue record for this title is available from the British Library.

ISBN: 978-1-83543-351-5

The opinions expressed in this book are the author's own and do not reflect the views of the publisher, author's employer, organisation, committee or other group or individual

First Published in 2025

**Olympia Publishers
Tallis House
2 Tallis Street
London
EC4Y 0AB**

Printed in Great Britain

# Dedication

To all those forcibly disappeared in the prisons of tyrants around the world.

"Why are we here? That is the question. And we are blessed that we happen to know the answer. Yes, in this immense confusion, one thing alone is clear. We are waiting for Godot to come...We are not saints, but we have kept our appointment."

**Waiting for Godot**
*Samuel Beckett*

# Chapter One
# The Walls Have Ears

As she sat on the edge of a wall overlooking the lively Umayyad Square, Sana couldn't help but feel a sense of contentment. Clad in a white dress embroidered with black and a green shawl draped over her head, she waited patiently for her friends to join her for the eight-p.m. play. Her thoughts, however, were far from the present moment. She was consumed by the literary works of Shakespeare, Browning, Milton, and Gordon—all of which were essential to her master's thesis on literature in the Renaissance period.

Despite the day's intellectual exertions, Sana still wore her white dress, seemingly inviting the challenges and hardships of the day to stain its pristine attire. She knew it was going to be a long and arduous day, yet she persisted with her white dress—a decision she would soon come to regret. As the sun rose on that fateful March morning in 2011, she chose her white dress over a calming blue one, unaware that the day's events would take a turn for the worse, drenching her in a torrential downpour that left the once-spotless attire stained and muddy.

Sana had agreed to attend the play at the theater with her friend Fatima despite feeling exhausted from a day of lectures at the university. The thought of sitting through a long and uncomfortable journey on the crowded white microbus, known as 'the mouse,' was enough to persuade her to stay in town for the night.

Perched on the wall's edge, Sana's eyes caught sight of a poster bearing the name of the play, *The Know-it-All,* written and directed by the esteemed Fayez Al-Asmar. The play was dubbed as 'experimental theater,' a trend that had gained popularity in recent years. Drawing inspiration from the Theatre of the Absurd, particularly Samuel Beckett's *Waiting for Godot,* the play piqued Sana's interest.

The phrase 'Waiting for Godot' echoed through her mind as she contemplated the play. The story's central focus revolves around characters living in a nihilistic existence, marginalized and isolated, awaiting the arrival of Godot to improve their lives. Despite the play's seemingly absurd plot, it held truth, especially in light of the current political climate in the region.

*The play may seem surreal, but it holds a mirror to the truth,* Sana mused. "Will Godot ever come to alleviate the suffering of the oppressed, uplift the marginalized, and break the isolation of those who are isolated?" In Beckett's play, Godot never arrives, and the problems persist without resolution. But in reality, Sana saw things differently.

The revolutionary movement in the Arab world was at its peak, with the fall of leaders like Zinedine Ben Ali in Tunisia and Hosni Mubarak in Egypt offering glimmers of hope. Perhaps there were solutions after all. Could the Arab Spring reach Syria, too? The recent chants and protests in Souk al-Hamidiya, which were quickly quashed by the security apparatus, hinted that it might.

Sana contemplated the idea that the play was absurd, yet it held so much truth in the current political climate. As a Syrian, she understood the inherent fear of the security services and intelligence personnel[1] who were disguised as civilians. She

---

[1] Famously known as the "mukhabarat". They are feared and firmly entrenched

knew that 'the walls have ears,' and she kept her thoughts to herself. She saw a man standing on the other side of the door, dressed in a black suit, shirt, and tie. She mistook him for security personnel due to their ubiquitous presence in the area. However, the contrast of black against his white skin gave her a sense of security, and she noticed him smiling at her.

Sana had a vivid imagination and enjoyed inventing stories about the people she encountered in her daily life. She would craft tales about anyone she met on the street, on the bus, at the university, in a cafe, or anywhere else.

*This man, an engineer at the Ministry of Agriculture, has four children and a modest salary that is not enough to pay his hundred-thousand-pound electricity bill. When he attempted to file a complaint, he was asked to pay first. Frustrated, he raised an objection.*

*This housewife was robbed this morning and is on her way to the police station to report the incident despite knowing that her purse and money will not be returned.*

*This young woman is in tears because she was forced into an engagement with a sixty-year-old man by her father. The man owns an apartment and a car and will pay her dowry in dollars, but she is unhappy with the arrangement.*

Sana's musings came to an end as Fatima arrived with a group of her friends from afar. After exchanging greetings, Fatima signaled for the young man dressed in black to approach.

---

institutions in all Syrian cities. President Bashar al-Assad, like his father before him, has used the surveillance of the mukhabarat to maintain his authoritarian grip. Unsubstantiated figures show that the mukhabarat employed either one in six or one in eight Syrians.

"Sana, this is my brother, Mansour. Mansour, this is Sana, the friend I told you about."

Sana was taken aback by the sudden revelation. Moments ago, he had been the security guard at the Opera House.

Fatima continued with the introduction: "Mansour is a lawyer working for Al-Afandi Law Firm, specializing in family affairs and domestic violence. Sana is an English literature graduate and is currently preparing for a master's thesis on the influence of the European Renaissance on English literature."

Both Sana and Mansour responded in unison, "It's a pleasure to meet you." The simultaneous response between the two lightened up the introduction and was followed by smiles and laughter that lasted throughout the evening.

The theater performance was mostly tedious, but Sana couldn't shake the thought of 'Godot' from her mind and its connection to the current events in the region and the raging Arab Spring. She wanted to discuss her thoughts with the group but quickly changed her mind. She realized that her views were in opposition to the Syrian regime and that someone in the group might report her to the relevant authorities.

# Chapter Two
# Aging Twenty Years in One Day

In the spring of 2011, the winds of the Arab Spring blew across the Syrian cities, igniting flames of protests in Daraa, Damascus, and eventually reaching Sana's city by the end of March. The demonstrations escalated in frequency, with the people demanding freedom and the overthrow of the regime. As more cities joined in, the Syrian government initiated a systematic campaign to quell the protests, accusing the demonstrators of foreign saboteurs while simultaneously branding them as terrorists.

The regime's brutal attacks caused the death of countless protesters, and as the situation in the country worsened, Sana was forced to discontinue her university studies. The roads were no longer safe, and the city was filled with security and intelligence checkpoints, leaving Sana with a mix of emotions: hope and despair, optimism and pessimism.

Then, on April 1, 2011, Douma had its first casualty. Sana, who had been a passive observer from her room window, became an active participant. She began to assist the injured as the bombing intensified. Her several First Aid courses back in high school were no match for the chaos she now faced. Sana needed more training.

She then met Dr. Imad, an emergency medicine specialist who worked at Damascus Central Hospital. With the onset of the demonstrations, Dr. Imad chose to abandon the safety of the hospital to treat those injured in the makeshift hospitals established by the protestors. Together with Sana, they formed an emergency medical team to treat the people in the city.

Dr. Imad was an essential figure in the chaotic and dangerous environment of Ghouta and Douma, where the Syrian regime had laid siege to the cities, preventing the entry of essential supplies such as medicine and food. Despite the dire situation, he was always able to procure what was necessary for the field hospital's operations. He had a network of suppliers who smuggled medical supplies into the cities, but for safety reasons, Dr. Imad referred to them using pseudonyms. He referred to them as 'Al-Shami, Al-Homsi, Al-Halabi, Al-Diri, Al-Idlibi, Al-Darawi, Al-Raqawi,' linking each name to a different Syrian city. Whenever a new city joined the movement, Dr. Imad added the name of a person from that city. Sana worked closely with Dr. Imad in planning and organizing the smuggling operations, and she would sometimes meet the suppliers to collect the much-needed medicine.

Sana was initially overwhelmed by the violence and the constant fear of bombings, but the critical need for medical supplies and the ever-increasing violence against civilians pushed her to overcome her fears. She worked tirelessly alongside Dr. Imad, learning everything she could from him and developing into a skilled nurse. She could now conduct clinical examinations, administer injections, suture wounds, and prescribe medication.

The field hospital's location constantly changed, and Sana and Dr. Imad moved from one basement to another, never staying in one place for too long, as bombs fell. Sana lived in danger, listening to the sounds of bombs, bullets, and bloodshed. Yet she always managed to stay safe. Instead, she only saw the aftermath as wounded and injured individuals came to her for treatment.

The field hospital became her home, and she moved with it, carrying her small bag and continuing to do her job, trying to focus on her tasks and separate them from the terrifying reality that surrounded her.

Sana had always felt that she was a survivor, someone who could withstand any obstacle that came her way. But when the field hospital she worked in was hit with ballistic missiles, all of her coping strategies were rendered useless. The explosion was deafening, and when the dust settled, Sana found herself surrounded by complete and utter devastation.

The eerie silence that followed the attack was unnerving. Body parts were scattered everywhere, and the building she was in had collapsed onto its inhabitants. Amidst the rubble, she saw a child's hand clutching a blood-stained stuffed bear, a severed foot and part of a bloody torso, and a dead father embracing his dead daughter. It was a scene of complete and utter destruction, one that would haunt her for the rest of her life.

Sana's survival was nothing short of a miracle. Although she couldn't hear anything, the screams and cries for help were visible to her. She saw the charred remains of Dr. Imad attached to one of the walls and identified him by the chain he wore around his neck. It took her a few moments to realize what had happened, but when she did, she was overcome with shock and grief.

Despite her own trauma, Sana ran to help the wounded. She came across a child writhing in pain, blood spurting from their head. In an effort to stop the bleeding, she placed her hand on the child's head but was horrified to find her hand sinking inside. Her fear was overwhelming, but she tried to pull her hand back to no avail. She carried the child and ran outside the destroyed building, not realizing the gate was open, and the door was split in two.

As she stepped outside, a man shouted, "Cover up, sister! Cover up!" Sana was not wearing a headscarf, and although she was not necessarily committed to wearing one, she covered her head with a light shawl to avoid harassment. The man, a stranger who worked in the ambulance team, had taken it upon himself to act as her guardian and prioritize asking her to cover her head, ignoring everything else. The audacity of it all...

Initially, Sana believed that she was unharmed. But as she continued to treat the wounded, the pain gradually made itself known. Her foot became weak and her hand heavy, but she kept working until she finally collapsed from exhaustion. Several shrapnel pieces had penetrated her hands and feet.

*Detachment was no longer possible.*

She wrote:

*That day was a terror. In an instant, I aged twenty years. I'm no longer the twenty-four-year-old who tried to distance herself from reality. At that moment, I realized that Godot would never arrive, and life would never be the same again.*

*I used to think that life was just a part of reality, something we experience every day without much thought. But that day, everything changed. The horrors of war had come crashing into my life, and I was forced to confront the reality of the situation.*

*Now, life has become a nightmare for me. It's like something out of a film or a TV show, but I'm living in this harsh reality. The memories of that day will stay with me forever, a constant reminder of the brutality and senselessness of war.*

# Chapter Three
# Paying It Forward

As an only child, Sana was the center of her parents' world. They would grant any request she made, but when the uprising began, her father, Abu Sana, urged her to move to the safety of either her uncle's house in the capital or her aunt's house in Hama. However, Sana remained steadfast in her decision to stay and help those in need. "I cannot abandon them. I must stay and make a difference," she responded firmly to her mother's attempts to persuade her.

"What's happening to the people of my city is happening to me," Sana declared. "I won't flee or leave behind my family, friends, and neighbors." Despite her mother's pleas, Sana remained determined, leaving them both stained with sadness.

Sana's conversations with her father were different. Having lived through the rule of President Hafez al-Assad in the 1980s, he understood the Syrian regime. He expressed his concern, warning her of the regime's criminal behavior that had ruined the lives of Syrians and turned the country into a farm. "I don't want you to become one of their victims," he said. "They have raped women, displaced children, and destroyed homes. You need to protect yourself."

However, Sana didn't engage in any exchanges that would lead to conflict. She simply replied, "I will not abandon my city."

Sana's father told a tale of Hama's past, particularly one he had heard in the 1980s. It was a gruesome one, told to him by an elderly woman named 'Umm Ihsan.' Umm Ihsan and her family had escaped from Hama to Douma years ago.

According to Umm Ihsan, after the attack on the city center of Hama, the shabiha[2], or pro-government militia, came to her home. They commented on the smell coming from outside, that of her seven children who had been set ablaze. One wryly said, "This is the reward for those who dare to attack the President." She recounted the atrocities she had witnessed, which included the rape and murder of young girls, as well as the desecration of corpses through burning, crucifixion, and dragging.

Umm Ihsan went on to describe a fourteen-year-old girl who had been buried under her family's bodies for three days. The shabiha had massacred her entire family, lining them up and shooting them. The girl fell alongside her parents and siblings but somehow managed to survive. For three days, she remained silent, fearing that if she called out for help, the shabiha would kill her. Fortunately, a woman heard her quietly moaning and rescued her from under the bodies.

The story moved Sana deeply but did not deter her from altering her plans—despite her mother's anxious objections and her father's fearful warnings. She resolved to live in makeshift hospitals in the basements, much to her mother's threat of severing ties with her and her father's disapproval of her decision. In the end, her parents grudgingly accepted her choice, but they lived in constant worry, knowing that the majority of the

---

[2] **Shabiha** is a term for state sponsored mercenaries of the Syrian government loyal to the Assad family. The mercenaries consist exclusively of Alawite men paid by the regime to eliminate figures of its domestic opposition and alleged fifth-columnists. Shabiha were established in the 1980s to smuggle weapons to the Syrian soldiers stationed in Lebanon during the Syrian occupation of Lebanon. However, post-2011 the term "Shabiha" is generally used as a generalized, insulting description of an Assad supporter.

city's inhabitants were vulnerable to mortars, missiles, and barrel bombs.

Abu Sana was well-known for his adage; 'Life is about paying it forward.' When Sana shared her intention to remain and work in field hospitals despite her father's objections, she frequently used this expression in their conversations. Her response remained unchanged: "Life is about paying it forward. I will strive to pay it forward in any way I can."

She later wrote:

*"I do not regret any moment of my life. I have always acted in accordance with my conscience.* Waiting for Godot *fueled my momentum, and even in the darkest moments when I thought he would never come, I did not lose hope. For me, hope is the very essence of life. Without hope, there can be no life at all."*

On the day the field hospital was bombed, news of the attack reached Sana's parents, causing them to fear for their daughter's safety. Rushing to the site, Abu Sana prepared himself for the worst while Sana's mother could not hold back her grief, crying out, "My only daughter is dead!"

Upon their arrival, the scene was one of chaos and devastation, with rubble and bodies scattered everywhere. Amidst the commotion, they frantically searched for any information about their daughter, pleading with anyone they could find. Graffiti on the walls proclaimed 'Freedom Forever' and 'Down with the Government,' while the sounds of screams and takbeers[3] filled the air.

---

[3] Takbeer is the utterance of 'Allahu akbar' which translates literally as "God is greatest" or "God is greater", and as is known as the Takbeer, playing a pivotal role in much of the Islamic faith. The phrase serves as a reminder to

Finally, they received an update from one of the doctors at a nearby field hospital. Sana's mother felt a sudden rush of blood to her head and began to feel dizzy as she waited to hear about her daughter's fate. "Your daughter is fine," the doctor said, giving them a glimmer of hope. "She was hit by some shrapnel, but she will be okay."

---

followers of Islam that no matter the situation or emotion, God is always greater than any real or imaginary entity.

# Chapter Four
# Perseverance

Sana lay on a creaky bed in the corner of the field hospital, enveloped in a once-white sheet that had now taken on a yellowish hue due to age. The space was abuzz with activity as doctors and nurses moved about, tending to the injured. The surgical equipment, comprising scissors, scalpels, threads, and needles, was within easy reach on the edge of the bed. As the medical team performed the critical surgery to remove the shrapnel from Sana's body, her hands and feet were wrapped in white gauze. Despite the lack of an operating room or sterile medical environment, the team deftly carried out the procedure with their limited resources, exhibiting admirable expertise.

*I wonder, where does this hatred stem from? How can individuals from the same nation engage in such atrocious acts against their fellow citizens and acquaintances? It is unfathomable to me. While I had previously heard about the regime's heinous practices and how prisoners were treated before the revolution, I never imagined it would escalate to this extent. What has become of these individuals? How have they forfeited their sense of humanity, morphing into ruthless beasts devoid of compassion? How can they find gratification in committing murder and inflicting harm on other humans?*

Approaching Sana's parents, the doctor spoke, "We have

removed as much shrapnel as possible given our limited resources here. Some cannot be removed at this time due to their precarious location, but the human body can adapt, and they will not pose a problem in the future."

Concerned, Abu Sana asked, "Will she be all right?"

Smiling, the doctor replied, "Yes, she just needs a little rest, and she'll be back to her old self, even better. Good health to you, Sana!"

Sana's mother was overwhelmed with a mix of relief and anxiety as she held her daughter lying on a bed in the field hospital, her hands and feet wrapped in gauze, bits of blood staining the sheets. Despite the chaos and clamor of the surroundings, she managed to stay composed for her daughter's sake.

Silencing her parents before they could lecture her, Sana vowed, "I must re-operate the field hospital once more. I won't let the efforts of Dr. Imad go to waste."

After a prolonged silence, broken only by her mother's sobs, Sana's father spoke, "The anguish we went through until we learned that you were safe was indescribable. Every time we encountered a lifeless body on the ground, my heart would stop beating with fear that it was you. Each moment felt like an eternity, as if I had lost you forever."

Sana readjusted her hijab, which the nurse had carefully placed on her head. The words of the paramedic still echoed in her mind, "Cover up, my sister, cover up!" Still, she was determined not to surrender. She refused to abandon her work or goals, driven by her desire to aid the people in her city. She was prepared to give it her all without hesitation. "I won't give up!" she declared with unwavering resolve.

*I did not want my parents to worry. They tried to convince me to abandon the idea of reopening the field hospital and leave the city for my own safety. They tried to motivate me, scare me, and even resort to crying and sobbing, but deep down, I knew what I had to do. They were convinced that I was determined to work on re-operating the hospital, and they were right. I had made up my mind, and that was the end of it.*

# Chapter Five
# Bird's Milk[4]

Re-establishing the field hospital was an uphill battle, one that required significant effort and resources, especially when it came to acquiring the necessary equipment and medicine. With the help of some local women, Sana revisited the site of the bombing and salvaged what was left of the equipment and medicine. She then set out to find a new location for the hospital, a suggestion made by the doctor who had treated her. The location, situated on a street overlooking Khurshid Street near Taha Mosque, was deemed a strategic spot by the doctor.

However, the task of obtaining the essential supplies proved to be the most pressing concern for Sana. Dr. Imad had dealt with suppliers using fake names, and their contact information was lost in the bombing. Despite her attempts to reach out to them through the numbers provided, Sana's efforts were in vain, leaving her with a sense of despair. She had met some of the suppliers but had no useful information about them, except for their aliases—Al-Raqawi and Al-Homsi.

Sana knew that without basic medicine and equipment, her efforts to run the hospital would be in vain. She was determined to acquire the materials. While she had arranged everything else, including working with the doctor who had treated her, training

---

[4] The proverb "bringing bird's milk" is commonly used to refer to accomplishing something that seems impossible or unattainable (e.g. Asking for the moon).

local women and girls in first aid, securing a suitable location, and moving the remaining equipment from the old hospital to the new location, the lack of supplies was a significant hindrance to her mission.

As her phone rang, Sana's heart skipped a beat. She hesitated before answering but eventually picked up the call. A voice on the other end introduced himself as Al-Shami and offered his condolences for the death of Dr. Imad in the bombing. Sana was surprised to hear from someone she didn't know but listened intently as Al-Shami explained that Dr. Imad had given him her number in case of an emergency. He was now calling to deliver the materials as promised.

Al-Shami assured Sana that he never expected to use the number and that he held Dr. Imad in high regard. The two agreed that the first batch of materials would arrive the following day, with Al-Shami himself delivering them to the square near Taha Mosque at ten o'clock in the morning. Sana was given instructions to enter Abu Saeed's shop on the corner of the mosque and ask about the weather. If he answered, "It will rain." Then it would be safe to move the equipment.

As the call ended, fear crept into Sana. She couldn't shake off the nagging feeling that Al-Shami might be a member of the Syrian regime or one of the many dangerous thugs who roamed the area. Sana spent a sleepless night, consumed by these worries.

Despite her fears, Sana resolved to go to Abu Saeed's shop the next morning. She had no alternative. Abu Saeed, a pious man in his sixties, was the owner and a trusted figure in the community. Sana could always count on finding whatever she needed at the shop. She remembered Abu Saeed's famous greeting to customers, "Your request is here, and if it isn't, I know someone who can get it for you, even if you're asking for bird's milk."

The mosque was a twenty-minute walk from her house, and Sana set off with a mix of hesitation and determination. When she arrived, she noticed a group of young men gathered at the door of the shop. Sana hesitated to enter while it was crowded and instead pretended to be waiting for someone. She checked the clock many times, hoping it would ease her suspicions and reduce any potential attention toward her. Eventually, the shop cleared out.

Sana moved cautiously. Many of the people in the market had spotted her, and some even knew her. She peered into the store through the glass front, but her view was obstructed. With quick steps, she crossed the street and entered the shop, which was nearly devoid of any merchandise. The siege had stripped most shops of their products, and checkpoints prevented anything from being brought in. Not even basic necessities like rice, lentils, bread, flour, gas, vegetables, or fruit were allowed. The groups of shabiha stationed at the checkpoints surrounding the city and at its entrances had a single message: *'Kneel to the regime or starve.'*

Her eyes scanned the almost empty shop, taking note of the sparsely stocked shelves and the few household items and cleaning supplies that remained. In a corner, she spotted a gas canister. Her heart sank as she realized it was unlikely that Abu Saeed, the usual shopkeeper, would have any bird's milk for her.

To her surprise, a young man in his twenties greeted her instead of Abu Saeed. She hesitated briefly, but her need for supplies urged her to speak up. "Peace be upon you. Where is Abu Saeed?"

The young man's reply shocked her to the core. "My father was killed in a bombing a few days ago. I am Saeed. How can I assist you?"

Despite her confusion, she resolved to stay. "When will it rain?"

A smile graced the young man's face as he responded, "Today. Come to the warehouse from here."

Sana descended the staircase, her body shaking and sweat pouring down her face. She quickly adjusted her hijab, which had slipped from the perspiration, and focused on counting the steps to calm her nerves. This was a technique Dr. Imad had taught her to cope with stress, telling her to 'occupy her mind with something else.' She had prepared for every possible scenario except for what came next.

She reached the bottom of the staircase, the dirty black-painted wooden boards creaking beneath her feet.

"Mansour!"

# Chapter Six
# Everything Will Be All Right

Sana had not seen Mansour since their evening back at the Opera House. His kind, gentle nature had still left a lasting impression on her. They exchanged information about their families and the situation in Syria. Initially, Sana had only planned to meet with Mansour, aka 'Al-Shami,' for a short time to obtain equipment for her mission, but they ended up speaking for hours.

Sana learned that Mansour had become one of the most prominent activists on the ground, working in humanitarian aid to provide medical equipment, medicine, and food to the people of Eastern Ghouta. His name became known as 'Mansour Al-Shami,' making him a target for the Syrian regime's intelligence services. Despite being relentlessly pursued, Mansour remained steadfast in his mission to help others, and he became a fugitive as a result.

Sana was grateful that Mansour had chosen to stay in Douma for a while, and she saw him as her own personal 'Godot.' She had been waiting for someone like him to help her with her mission, and now he was there, seeking her help in finding a way forward.

Without hesitation, Mansour agreed to join Sana at the field hospital. As they worked together, their mutual affection became increasingly apparent. However, they both recognized that practicality took precedence over emotions in their current circumstances, and they focused their energies on their work at the hospital.

Their daily routine was overwhelming, with constant bombings and new tragedies each day. In the evenings, they would sit at the door of the field hospital, sipping tea or coffee and pondering the difficult questions of what the future held for them.

"How will our lives be after all of this?" Sana asked Mansour one evening.

"It seems that we will die here," Mansour responded.

Sana's anger flared up at his response. She refused to give up hope and surrender to the situation they found themselves in. Despite the overwhelming odds against them, she held on to her aspirations for the future, determined to see them through.

Mansour couldn't help but notice the tight veil wrapped around Sana's head. It was a far cry from the first time they met when she wore a light shawl and her dark tresses danced in the breeze. "I didn't know you wore a hijab?" he inquired.

"It wasn't my choice," Sana responded with a resigned tone. "The situation demands it."

Mansour understood all too well the volatile climate they lived in. Extremism and manipulation had become the norm, as religious opportunists vied for power while the regime played a double game of presenting themselves as guardians of secularism and pluralism. The result was a society torn apart by intolerance and violence, with Mansour and Sana trapped in the middle of it all.

As the siege tightened and supplies dwindled, Mansour suggested traveling to the capital for aid, but Sana refused. "It's too dangerous. They'll arrest you," she warned.

Mansour was frustrated, but Sana had a plan. Unbeknownst to him, she had already arranged for a trip to the capital to secure supplies. "I've made arrangements with smugglers to get through the checkpoints. I'll be back in two days," she declared with determination.

Mansour was taken aback by her bravery, but he couldn't help but worry about her safety. "Are you sure it's worth the risk?" he asked.

"I have to try," Sana responded firmly. "I refuse to give up and let them win. We have to keep fighting."

"But it's dangerous; I can't let you go," Mansour said, worried.

"Mansour, the matter is settled. Please don't make it harder," Sana said firmly.

Mansour couldn't shake off the feeling of uncertainty. What would happen to them if she didn't return? But he knew that Sana was a force to be reckoned with, and he trusted her determination to keep pushing forward against all odds.

"See you in two days," Sana said, hugging Mansour. Mansour held her, breathing in her scent, feeling her warmth, unwilling to let go.

Sana had always been mindful of the region's customs and traditions, especially after the recent rise of Islamist militancy and the resulting stricter restrictions. But in that moment, all of that was pushed aside as she clung to Mansour, tears streaming down her face. She whispered in his ear, "Don't worry, everything will be okay." Mansour knew that Sana was trying to reassure herself more than him. He couldn't bear the thought of losing her, but he knew she was strong and determined to find a solution. He held onto her, savoring every moment until they had to part.

# Chapter Seven
# The State and Its Master

Sana didn't encounter any security issues at first, but this changed once she reached Harasta. Her original plan was to walk from Douma to Harasta to meet with a smuggler. The trip was only five kilometers, but in reality, she had to skirt countless checkpoints by trudging through farms and bushes, dressed in an abaya and veil to hide her identity. Those five miles ended up taking her over five hours, with heavy rain and her attire hindering her progress. The journey was both exhausting and tiring, and she was relieved to have the smuggler as her guide.

Despite the significant delay, Sana went to rest for a few hours at her friend's house in Harasta. However, due to the significant delays, she only had half an hour to rest. She decided to take off her hijab and put on regular clothing instead of the abaya.

As Sana boarded the microbus at two-thirty p.m., she chose to sit at the back to avoid drawing any suspicion. Her first hurdle was the checkpoint at the entrance to the city of Harasta, but the personnel were occupied with another vehicle, and the microbus passed without inspection. Sana felt a wave of relief, hoping that the rest of the journey would be smooth with no other checkpoints.

As she caught her breath, Sana began to weave imaginary stories about the other passengers on the microbus, but this time, her stories were filled with terror. She imagined stories of the horrific violence and tragedies faced by the passengers.

*She imagined a sixty-year-old woman carrying a baby who lost her daughter in a bombing and whose infant granddaughter was wounded by shrapnel. The woman was now on her way to the hospital for treatment. Another passenger was a man in his forties whose house was destroyed in the bombing, killing his parents. Despite trying to save them, he was only able to find his mother's hand, identified by the ring on her finger. The rest of her body was still buried under the rubble, and his father's body was charred, so he buried them together. Yet another passenger was a twenty-year-old girl who was kidnapped from the Salihiya area in Damascus and sold to one of the checkpoints surrounding Douma. The checkpoint personnel took turns to rape her before throwing her out naked. She managed to gather some clothes from a nearby house and was now on her way home.*

Unfortunately, these imaginings were all too real.

Suddenly, the microbus stopped near Al-Taqwa Mosque, and the checkpoint personnel commanded everyone to present their ID cards. Sana was so lost in her thoughts that she didn't realize what was happening until the officer shouted, "Hey! Don't you understand? Your ID card, now!'"

Sana's mind wandered as the officer held onto her ID card. She was lost in thought until the officer called out her name. "Sana Assali, please come with us," he shouted. With a sense of dread, Sana stepped off the microbus, hoping to appear confident. She had prepared herself for this moment and was determined to respond to any questions from the officer with a firm 'it must be some kind of mistake.'

Her heart was pounding, and her body was drenched in sweat

as she followed the officer. She was consumed by fear, wondering if they knew about her plans and whether they would arrest her or cause her harm. The officer led her to a small tent with 'United Nations' written on it. Inside, she was surprised to see Lieutenant Ahmed Al-Ali, her high school classmate, sitting on a sofa. He greeted her with a smile and said, "Welcome, Sana, I see you're in our neck of the woods."

Relief washed over her as she realized that Ahmed had summoned her for a conversation. It was clear that neither he nor the officers were aware of her plans or the nature of her work. This was a good sign. 'Hello Ahmed, I am on my way to my uncle's house,' Sana said, trying to keep her composure.

Ahmed gestured for her to sit on the opposite sofa under the United Nations canopy. The furniture must have been looted from one of the cities in Eastern Ghouta. Looting operations were common, and the regime's security apparatus, army, and shabiha violated public and private property. They either sold them in second-hand markets or used them in their homes or, in this case, in their tents.

Sana reluctantly sat down, wanting the meeting to end quickly. She wondered what Ahmed wanted from her. Ahmed proceeded to speak about the state and its master, terrorists, and infiltrators. He discussed biased TV channels and the opposition bullies. He continued, speaking about their mission to cleanse the country of germs as entrusted to them by the President. He praised the heroic operations of the Syrian regime army, who had given their most precious belongings for the sake of their homeland and their master. Ahmed also talked about the corrective movement and the celebrations that would take place that day. He emphasized that the year 2013, which was only a month away, would be the year of complete purification. They would purify the country from all traitors and insurgents.

Sana nodded her head in agreement as Ahmed finished his lecture on patriotism and the supposed mission to cleanse the country of traitors and insurgents. Despite her feigned compliance, a flurry of questions continued to churn inside her head. How could her old classmate and the other regime officers carry out such heinous acts against their own people, friends, and even their own kin?

As Ahmed wrapped up his speech with a pointed question, Sana felt the urge to lash out at him, to tell him what she really thought of their regime. But she held back, knowing the danger she was in. Instead, she replied calmly, "Yes, of course."

Feeling both relieved and disappointed, Sana made her way back to the microbus, hoping to put this harrowing encounter behind her.

## Chapter Eight
## A Funeral Car

On their journey back to the countryside, Sana knew that transporting medical supplies was a dangerous endeavor. Checkpoints, manned by both regime army and sectarian militias, conducted extensive inspections on vehicles leaving Damascus. To avoid suspicion, Sana planned to travel in a funeral car that made regular trips to deliver bodies to and from the capital city. The owner had promised to inform Sana of the date of his next trip, allowing her to accompany him.

Abu Hamid, the driver of the funeral car, was transporting a man who had passed away from a heart attack from Al-Asadi Hospital in Damascus to the town of Mesraba. Sana had only arrived less than a day ago, but already, death from natural causes had become a luxury. She had split the medicine into two bundles, tightly wrapping the first and placing it beneath the corpse in the coffin. Slabs of ice were tied around the body to prevent decomposition and smell. Sana had taped the second bundle, which contained small medical equipment such as gauze, cotton, needles, and more, tightly around her stomach and feet.

As they neared Harasta, the initial checkpoints on the outskirts of Damascus conducted only cursory inspections. Despite this, Abu Hamid, their driver, was on high alert. At any moment, he may need to offer bribes to officers to ensure their safe passage. Each time they approached a checkpoint, he handed an envelope containing the required passage fee to the officer in charge, and then they continued on their way. While some of the checkpoint personnel physically inspected the car, none interfered with the coffin or Sana, who sat alone in the back. Abu Hamid, always the reassuring presence, turned to Sana at every checkpoint and said, "Do not be afraid, miss. It will be easy, God willing."

Abu Hamid was a man in his forties, gentle in both his appearance and demeanor. His smile, which never seemed to leave his face, was a welcome sight in their tense journey. Before the protests in Syria disrupted commercial movement, he made trips and tours transporting goods between the Gulf countries and Syria. With few options left, he had turned to driving small cars to make ends meet for his family. He had a wife who was pregnant with their third child, and they all lived together in one house in Jaramana, on the outskirts of Damascus. Sana made sure that he received his full wages, knowing how important it was for him to provide for his family.

The car came to a stop at the checkpoint on the Southern Highway, where a bus was also being searched. Abu Hamid got out of the car and approached the officer in charge, who accepted the envelope containing the passage fee. However, some of the sectarian militias seemed displeased with how the sharing of the fees was being conducted.

Suddenly, one of the militia members ordered Abu Hamid and Sana to step out of the car and stand against a wall with several other bus passengers. While weapons were loaded around them, the group was subjected to a rigorous search. The officers searched the bus and car thoroughly but did not open the coffin.

Although the vehicle inspections had come to a close, the checkpoint personnel continued to torment the bus passengers. They were made to stand against a wall for over two hours while being verbally assaulted with the most degrading of terms by the checkpoint officer, who referred to them as 'conspirators,' 'terrorists,' and 'insects.'

After two hours of humiliation, the officers split the group into two—men on the left and women on the right. The men were subjected to a thorough search, during which the officers found lighters, cigarette packs, keys, mobile phones, and money. They returned the belongings, but the officer kept the money.

The checkpoint officer then posed a question before releasing the group: who they supported. When the group whispered, "Mr. President," he loaded his weapon, and the other personnel followed suit. He asked again, but the group's response was still too low to hear. "I can't hear you," he said and fired several shots in the air.

Finally, the group shouted at the top of their lungs, "Mr. President!" Fortunately, the women were not searched at that checkpoint, including Sana.

The car rolled down the deserted road, its engine purring steadily, but the weight of recent events hung heavy on both Sana and Abu Hamid. Neither spoke, lost in their own thoughts. Sana cracked open the car window, letting the icy air invade the vehicle. The putrid scent of the corpse in front of her seeped in as well, made worse by the melted ice that dripped into the car's interior. Sana tried to dry the floor with rags from the back of the car, but it was a futile effort. She had seen too many corpses lately, friends and acquaintances, but the tightly sealed bag beneath the body offered some solace that many lives would be saved.

Despite the fear and terror that accompanied them at every checkpoint, they passed the remaining ones on their way to Mesraba without incident. There were moments when Sana regretted her journey and longed for her loved ones, Mansour and her parents. The past two days had felt like an eternity, but as they approached the outskirts of Mesraba, she began to relax. Soon, she would reach Douma.

At last, they reached Mesraba, and Sana parted ways with Abu Hamid. She contacted an acquaintance in the area who offered her a place to stay for the night. Tomorrow, she would set off toward Douma, another chapter in her journey.

# Chapter Nine
# The Outskirts of Douma

Sana postponed the last leg of her journey to the outskirts of Douma because the safety situation in the area was dire. News of intensified bombings, sieges, and the deployment of regime elements, militias, and shabiha cast a dark cloud over her. She remained in Mesraba for three days, consulting with her connections to ensure her safe passage. On the fourth day, a young man named Ahmed volunteered to guide her. He was well-versed in the roads and knew how to avoid checkpoints and shabiha sites. Together, they planned to cover four kilometers over a span of five hours, taking breaks as needed. Sana carried a bag of medicine and equipment, while Ahmed carried the other.

As they set out, the sky was painted black by heavy rain-filled clouds. During their first hour of walking, they exchanged stories to pass the time. Ahmed spoke of his diabetic mother, his deceased father, and his married sister living abroad. Sana told him about Mansour, her parents, the field hospital, and the city she hailed from.

Ahmed led Sana to a small deserted farm near the Mesraba Bridge, which belonged to his uncle before it was ransacked by the shabiha. The two rested there for half an hour before continuing their journey toward Sana's destination. They walked parallel to the 2km main road, which was heavily guarded by checkpoints and military barracks. The sounds of bombing were within earshot, and they had even entered the city's district.

As they approached the outskirts of the city, Sana felt a sense of anticipation for her long-awaited reunion with Mansour and her parents. Ahmed promised to take her to the last point before the destination, where they parted ways. Sana carried her bags and continued on her journey alone, unaware of the danger that lay ahead.

Soon after, Sana was ambushed by a group of regime soldiers who surrounded her, heavily armed and shouting, "What are you doing here?" Ahmed watched from afar, unable to help her for fear of being killed himself. Sana froze in place, feeling hopeless as her life flashed before her eyes.

The shabiha opened her bags and accused her of treating terrorists, beating her with their hands, feet, and guns. She curled up on the ground, surrendering to the blows until the group's commanding officer arrived and ordered them to stop. He directed Sana to the car, where the driver helped her up.

The officer said, "Abu Azab[5], take this bitch who is treating terrorists." Abu Azab greeted Sana with a forceful slap, causing her to wince in pain and cover her eyes with a dirty cloth. The putrid odor in the air made it difficult for her to breathe as they pushed her into the back seat of the car and drove her away.

---

[5] Abu Azab translates to "Father of torture". Most political prisoners in Syria are arrested by members of the security forces, not the criminal police. Several networks of security forces still operate in Syria, and they hold wide powers of arrest and detention. The individuals who run the torture operations go by intimidating names such as "Abu Azab".

# Chapter Ten
# Keep Your Eyes Down

Sana was in a state of complete disorientation as she embarked on the hour-long journey. She had no idea where they were headed, as the voices outside the car were silent about their destination. Her mind was scattered, and she hoped that it was all just a terrible nightmare from which she would soon awaken. Throughout the journey, she was instructed to keep her eyes down, which she did without protest.

Upon arriving at the branch, Sana was once again subjected to physical abuse. She did not see it coming this time as her eyes were closed. Abu Azab himself slapped her as soon as she stepped out of the car. Others also mistreated her, spitting on her and pushing her, and then someone put her in a headlock. Abu Azab placed his heavy hand on her shoulder, almost causing her to collapse. He then led her into a building. She could feel the dampness of the place.

Sana found herself in a small room with only a chair, and Abu Azab shouted at her, "Take off your clothes." She looked at him defiantly, and he slapped her again, not once but twice, and shouted, "Take off your clothes." Sana reluctantly began to undress until she was left only in her underwear. He shouted again, "Take off your clothes," followed it with a slap and a punch.

Feeling humiliated and scared, Sana covered her body with her hands as Abu Azab ordered her to kneel down. She complied with his demand and knelt before him, even as he repeated the command three times. Afterward, he told her to get dressed, blindfolded her, and led her to a dark cell without uttering a word. It was later revealed that this degrading inspection was routinely conducted on all detainees to ensure that they were not hiding anything on their bodies, especially in the anus.

Sana had heard of the regime's solitary confinement cells for women, and now she found herself trapped in one. The cell was tiny, measuring just two meters long and one meter wide, with no ventilation except for a small hole in the door. A faint beam of light filtered in through the door and the hole, casting dim shadows on the walls. To her right was a narrow bed with a thin blanket, while to her left was a water tap that flowed directly into a foul-smelling toilet hole. A rusted bowl lay on the floor. The walls were covered in indecipherable graffiti, with a few bloodstains here and there.

The dampness of the cell crept into Sana's bones, and the dim light made her eyes strain to adjust. She tried to sleep, but the cold was too much to bear, and the screams of other prisoners in nearby cells made it impossible to rest. The cold ravaged her body. She took off her shoes and used them as a pillow under her head, tossing and turning in an attempt to sleep, but her eyes would not close. The sounds of torture echoed throughout the night, lasting until dawn.

In the morning, a guard opened the door and tossed in a plate of boiled eggs and bread, but Sana didn't eat. In the evening, another guard replaced the plate with a piece of hardened cheese and bread, but Sana still refused to eat.

As the night wore on, Sana's mental fortitude began to crumble. She felt frustrated, desperate, and terrified; her mind was plagued with memories of warnings and pleas from her parents and Mansour. Despite her best efforts to banish these thoughts, they continued to haunt her, and she struggled to find any solace.

A man entered her cell the next morning and gestured for her to follow him. Sana put on her shoes and walked behind him while a second officer followed behind her. She tried to look up and observe her surroundings, but the officer barked, "Keep your eyes on the floor!"

As they walked, Sana sensed the presence of many people around her, but she didn't dare to look up. The officer knocked on a door. A voice replied, "Enter."

He said to her, "Lieutenant-Colonel Fouad is waiting for you."

Sana entered the room and lifted her gaze from the floor for the first time. A small desk with a telephone stood before her, and a large man in a military uniform sat behind it. Two chairs were in front of the desk, one of which was broken. Behind the man hung two large portraits, one of the late President (the father) and the other of the current President.

Sana's worst fears had come true. She was now locked up in one of the regime's solitary confinement cells for women. The cell was nothing more than a dark, tiny, and dingy hole that measured only two meters by one meter. It was suffocating, with no ventilation except for a small hole in the door that let in a faint beam of light. The walls were covered in indecipherable graffiti, and a few bloodstains here and there suggested that the cell had seen its fair share of horror.

To her right, there was a narrow bed with a thin blanket that offered no warmth against the cold. To her left, there was a water tap that flowed directly into a foul-smelling toilet hole, with a rusted bowl lying on the floor. Sana tried to sleep, but the cold and the screams of other prisoners made it impossible to rest. She was freezing, and her body ached with every passing minute.

The guards would occasionally bring her food, but Sana didn't touch it. She was too afraid to eat, and the thought of consuming anything that came from the hands of her captors made her stomach churn.

As time passed, Sana's mental state deteriorated. She felt isolated, helpless, and afraid. She had no idea how long she would be locked up, and the thought of never seeing her family again made her heartache. Memories of her parents and Mansour flooded her mind, and she struggled to keep them at bay.

On the second day, a guard arrived and motioned for her to follow him. She put on her shoes and walked behind him while another guard followed close behind. They walked for what seemed like an eternity, and Sana could sense that they were surrounded by many people, but she kept her eyes down as instructed.

The guard knocked on a door, and a voice from inside replied, "Enter." The guard motioned for Sana to stand up, and after a brief moment, he returned to her and said, "Lieutenant-Colonel Fouad is waiting for you."

Sana entered the room and lifted her gaze from the floor for the first time. The room was sparsely furnished, with a small desk and telephone in front of her. Behind the desk sat a large man in a military uniform. Two chairs were in front of the desk, one of which was broken. Two portraits hung on the wall behind the man—one of the late President—the father—and the other of the current President.

The officer gestured to Sana to take a seat, and she perched on the edge of the chair, keeping her gaze fixed on the floor. She knew better than to give the officer a reason to be hostile toward her. The officer sifted through the papers in his hand before asking, "Do you enjoy treating terrorists?" Sana remained silent, fully aware that any response could be used against her. The officer stood up, strode toward her, and took a seat next to her. With his hand, he lifted her chin, forcing her to look him in the eye. "Answer!" he barked. Despite her desire to reply, Sana's tongue was tied. The words simply refused to come out.

Just as the tension in the room reached its peak, the phone rang, cutting through the thick silence. The officer jumped up to answer it. "Yes, yes, sir, yes, sir," he said before hanging up. With a press of the button, the officer called in his colleague, who promptly escorted Sana out of the room. As she was leaving his office, he told Sana, "I'll see you in the evening."

As they walked back to her cell, Sana dared to glance up and was greeted with the sight of a young man hanging by his hands, blood streaming from his feet. A naked girl stood in the corner, her body bearing signs of torture. The horrors of the place had finally begun to sink in.

# Chapter Eleven
# The Khatib Branch

As the evening descended, Lieutenant Colonel Fouad summoned Sana to his office. The mood in the room was immediately palpable, and Sana sensed that something was not quite right. Fouad did not invite her to sit but instead stood with an air of intimidation, his eyes fixed on Sana. He demanded, "Who are your partners?" Sana remained tight-lipped, refusing to confess to any accomplices. In response, Fouad threatened her, "If you don't confess to all your accomplices, I will make all the members of the branch take turns to rape you!"

Sana remained composed and steadfast in her silence. Fouad walked up to her and placed his hand on her face, his tone of voice taking a more intimate turn. "Listen, Sana," he said. "You are the one who determines your stay with us. Rest assured that it will be a long period, and you will either pass it in peace or face serious consequences."

Finally, Sana found her voice and spoke up for herself. "I didn't do anything wrong. All I did was treat civilians," she said, holding her ground. But instead of listening to her plea, Fouad flew into a rage and slapped her, calling her a 'whore' and insisting that the civilians she treated were actually terrorists.

Sana never saw Fouad again, but his orders were followed to the letter. For a month, she was subjected to daily torture sessions that almost took her life. Each night, she was dragged out of her cell and subjected to new forms of physical and psychological torture. She was raped, abused, and insulted, all while Fouad's officers laughed, drank, smoked, and treated her like nothing more than an object.

Sana's time in captivity was a living nightmare. Each day, she was subjected to the officers' carefully planned torture regime as if they were following a set curriculum. They relentlessly worked to break her spirit and force her to confess to a crime she did not commit.

The torture chamber was a bleak and desolate place, with nothing but a chair, a lamp, and walls painted in a faded gray. Sana sat on the chair, trying to steel herself against the horrors she knew were coming. As soon as the guards changed shifts, five masked officers entered the room, and the torture began.

The officers beat her savagely, using their hands, feet, and batons to strike every inch of her body. They hurled insults and accusations at her, calling her a terrorist, a whore, and a slut. Sana endured their cruel punishment until she passed out or was near death.

When she lost consciousness, the officers tied her up and hung her from the ceiling, dousing her with water to wake her up so that they could continue their onslaught. As the torture dragged on, new officers replaced those who grew tired, and the cycle continued.

After the final blow and failed attempts to wake Sana with water, the officers dragged her back into solitary confinement. This cycle continued every day.

*I didn't feel much pain despite the continuous beating they inflicted upon me. It was strange, as with the first flick or punch, my body started to desensitize, and the pain gradually faded away. I couldn't feel any sensation of pain, swelling, redness, or sores. It was as if my brain shut off after the first blow, and the pain was disappearing.*

The second stage of torture began in the second week. The sessions' length decreased, only occurring in the evenings, but their brutality increased. The physical abuse no longer consisted solely of beatings and verbal abuse. Instead, they stripped her of her clothing and left her vulnerable in a putrid-smelling chamber. A table was in the room, adorned with glasses of arak and mezze, and the torturers were unmasked this time. It seemed they had resolved to eliminate her entirely to prevent any chance of her identifying them.

As they sat around the table, the men talked about football, soap operas, and films while drinking alcohol. They made sure to sprinkle their conversation with insults and threats aimed at the extremist terrorists and saboteurs who they thought had destroyed their country and lives. Meanwhile, Sana was restrained by her hands and feet, naked, and subject to hours of sexual assault. As they drank, they took turns assaulting her, with one man on top of her moaning loudly while the others carried on as if nothing was happening.

*They took turns raping me. They were like animals with their stench. But my mind tried to protect me by imagining different images that could transport me to other places, taking me outside of my body.*

In the third level of torture, the cruelty reached new heights. It was executed in a series of installments. On the first day, the torturers pulled out Sana's nails and some of her teeth, leaving her bloodied body in her cell for three days without any food. On the fifth day, they tied her naked to the ceiling and hung weights from her nipples, taking turns playing with the weights to intensify the pain. Then, they gathered around her and urinated on her.

The fourth level of torture was different, as the victim's body could no longer bear any physical torture, and the torturers were not directed to kill her. As a result, they had to resort to other methods to inflict pain and suffering.

The torture began with psychological methods. A woman and her daughter were brought before her, and their hair burned. Their heads were then hit with a huge book to put out the fire. A young man was tied up and forced to drink large amounts of water, unable to urinate. Another young man was kicked repeatedly in the nose and mouth until they cracked. They forced a father to rape his son, all of which was accompanied by laughter and jokes.

*Each day was a battle, and I felt like death was hovering over me. It was difficult to comprehend how anyone could derive pleasure from such evil acts. I questioned how these people could return to their homes, play with their children, and treat their families and friends. These thoughts swirled around in my mind, but I couldn't find any satisfactory answers. The only conclusion that made sense to me was that they were not of this world; perhaps they were extraterrestrial beings.*

After enduring a month of torture, Sana was transferred to a crowded dormitory with other women and children. The living conditions were cramped, but the women took turns caring for her and providing comfort. Sana struggled to regain her senses, often waking up disoriented and muttering to herself before passing out again. She lost over fifteen kilograms of weight in just five weeks, but as time passed, her wounds began to heal, and her mind slowly cleared.

She observed the surroundings and noticed the damp, crusty walls and musty-smelling, worn-out blankets on the floor. There were three small rooms in the corner, two with toilet holes and a small tap. One room was used to store shoes, while the second was designated for defecation. The third room served as a shower, but the plastic curtains were worn out, offering little privacy.

As Sana got to know the women and children in the dormitory, she listened intently to their stories. One woman in her sixties had been arrested to pressure her son, a member of the Free Army, to surrender. Another woman and her three sons were detained at a checkpoint after a WhatsApp group on her phone called 'Al-Thawra[6]' was discovered. A third woman was accused of treating 'terrorists[7]' when she went to collect her passport and was subsequently arrested. One woman had rejected an officer's sexual advances, leading to her arrest, while the rest had suffered similar injustices.

Sana wished she could rewrite their stories with happy endings, but she knew it wasn't possible. She learned that she was being held at the Al-Khatib branch of the State Security, named after the neighborhood where it was located. Situated on Baghdad Street near the Red Crescent building, she had heard of the brutal practices of its members and officers but never imagined she would experience them firsthand.

---

[6] Al-Thawra translates to "revolution", which automatically connotes opposition to the government. The Syrian regime detained people for expressing their opinions both online and on the ground.

[7] The Syrian regime uses the word 'terrorists' to refer to all those who demand the change of the Syrian regime, in order to slander all dissidents as terrorists, making it easier to justify their torture and murder.

# Chapter Twelve
# The List of Heroines

Sana's body was no longer able to withstand the unrelenting abuse inflicted upon it. Her tormentors subjected her to more frequent and brutal torture sessions, causing her to lose consciousness frequently. Every Thursday, Sana and a group of girls were taken to Shabeh[8] Square, where their hands were bound with ropes, and they were beaten mercilessly with fists and sticks. The officers hurled insults at them, degrading them with names like 'whores,' 'sluts,' and 'terrorists' and accusing them of plotting against the president. The officers would beat the girls unconscious and urinate on them before leaving.

Sadly, some of the women in the dormitory never escaped the torture, and their lifeless bodies were often removed during the night. To honor these women, the others in the dormitory kept a secret record of their names, which they called 'The List of Heroines.' They carefully guarded the list from the officers, fearing that its discovery would bring more harm to them. When a prisoner was released, they would take the list with them to

---

[8] The infamous al **Shabeh torture** method is common in the Syrian Regime's detention centers. The detainee's hands are tied behind his/her back, then they're raised by the same rope which is tied to rings fixed to the ceiling, leaving the body suspended from the ground so the full weight is hanging from the wrists. This leads to dislocation of the shoulders and the rupture of the muscles in the shoulders and upper arms, and severe swelling of the hands. Detainees are often left this way for hours or days. This shabeh position is the most widespread and commonly used during torture.

inform the families of the deceased women. Then, the responsibility of maintaining the list would pass on to the next woman who left the prison.

*I can't bring myself to have faith in Godot's arrival. It's as if this world has no room for him, and these monsters who call themselves humans have blocked every possible entrance, leaving no space for him to enter. But even as hope dwindles and the darkness threatens to engulf us, I can't give up. The women who have perished in this living nightmare cannot have died in vain. I will persist and resist and fight until the very end.*

Throughout the week, Sana tended to her wounds and those of other women, doing her best to help care for their children. Despite the dire circumstances, she clung to hope. In a small corner of the dormitory, she fashioned a puppet theater out of blankets and shoes to entertain the children. Using spoons for hands and legs, she spun tales of hope, joy, and a brighter future, doing her best to revive the children's imagination, even if only for a little while.

Sana also organized educational sessions for the children, teaching them basic reading, writing, and math skills. With only rudimentary tools at her disposal, she wrote on the walls with small stones, encouraging the children to do the same to practice their lessons. She taught them to do math in their heads since there were no pens or paper available, as well as letters and verbs.

In a different part of the country, Umm Abboud, a conservative woman in her sixties, had fled Hama after her entire family was killed by the regime during the events of the 1980s. She now resided in the countryside of Damascus, swapping stories with others about the past and present. Despite the passage of time, the situation under both the father's and the son's rule remained largely unchanged. In the 1980s, unspeakable crimes were committed under the father's regime, with entire families executed in Hama, including Umm Abboud's own. Men had their beards set on fire, women were raped and executed, and children were slaughtered. The streets were strewn with corpses, and nobody dared to bury them. Eastern Ghouta suffered similar atrocities, with killings, bombings, arrests, executions, and liquidations.

Despite their differences, Sana and Umm Abboud engaged in extensive discussions on a wide range of topics, from politics and current events to personal histories and shared experiences. The ongoing situation in their country was a recurring theme, with a particular focus on the narrative put forth by the Syrian regime. The topic of terrorism and infiltrators was also frequently debated, with a shared agreement that the regime's practices embodied terrorism, while any actions taken by others were merely reactions.

Sana's experience was especially harrowing. She spent a year and a half in the Al-Khatib branch, bidding farewell to many of her fellow detainees, some of whom passed away while others were eventually released. The ever-mounting death toll meant that the list of casualties was updated frequently.

*The list of heroines was not something we created lightly. It was a tribute to the women who had lost their lives in that terrible place. If your name appeared on the list, or if you were chosen to carry it, you were considered a heroine—either one who had made the ultimate sacrifice or one who had survived. We repeated these words, not to convince ourselves of their truth, but to remind ourselves that our lives had value and that hope persisted despite everything.*

## Chapter Thirteen
## Lieutenant Colonel Said

During the final six months of Sana's detention at the Al-Khatib branch, Lieutenant Colonel Saeed replaced Lieutenant Fouad as the detainees' new supervisor. Sana caught Saeed's attention, and he began inviting her to his office for coffee from time to time.

On their first meeting, Sana was taken aback by the view outside of Saeed's office window, which overlooked a small green yard. The symmetry of the greenery and the gentle shadows of the tree branches gave her a sense of comfort. When he opened the window, a soft, refreshing breeze wafted in, something Sana had not experienced for months. The scent of moist soil filled her lungs, adding to the experience.

"Tell me about yourself, Sana," Saeed asked.

Initially, Sana hesitated. However, the appeal of his office, with its window overlooking the small garden and the aroma of coffee, enticed her to speak, albeit briefly. Saeed continued to summon Sana at least once a week to grow closer to her, but she refused his advances. Although she was open to speaking and exchanging ideas, she was determined not to fall prey to a relationship with her captor.

Sana was well aware of how victims could become attached to their captors and justify their actions. She reminded herself repeatedly that no one, including herself, could justify the atrocities committed by the regime against civilians.

Sana was faced with a difficult predicament. Declining Lt. Colonel Saeed's invitation to his office would result in his coercion for her attendance. Conversely, agreeing to his request would signal his power over her and ultimately lead to her compliance with his every whim. Therefore, Sana resolved to visit him only of her own volition and accord to avoid being forced to visit his office, creating a balance in dynamics.

Despite the numerous enticements offered by Saeed, such as a more comfortable environment that would entail better meals, coffee, and a cessation of torture, Sana adamantly refused to succumb to him physically. She only engaged in conversation, cognizant that her captor was capable of rape, as other prisoners had experienced under his colleagues' authority. Sana held firm that any physical submission would occur solely without her consent.

Thankfully, unlike his fellow officers, Lt. Colonel Saeed refrained from forcing himself upon Sana. Although he made attempts to draw nearer to her on various occasions, he kept a respectful distance between them, and their weekly meetings persisted.

In the midst of one of their meetings, Saeed posed a provocative query to Sana, "Why do you consort with terrorists? From your file, I am almost certain that you are secular and not one of the extremists, and we are a secular country?"

Sana was deeply affronted by the question but held her ground, unbothered by the potential consequences. "The regime you claim is secular is, in fact, a corrupt and criminal system based on nepotism and thuggery. Can the bombing of cities and towns with barrel bombs be called secular? Is the looting of people's livelihoods and the arrest and rape of women secular? There is nothing secular about that!"

Surprisingly, Saeed allowed Sana to continue speaking. She elucidated that those labeled as terrorists were, in fact, ordinary citizens who had lost everything. "A secular system should respect the beliefs of others and allow everyone to express their opinions," she added.

Sana expounded that the current regime had suppressed voices and enabled extremism for half a century. "This is not a secular system. This is an authoritarian regime," she concluded.

After delivering her impassioned speech, Sana was overcome with regret. She feared the dire consequences that might follow. Would her words only invite more torture, rape, or even death? She wondered why she spoke up when it would not change anything.

Saeed motioned for the guard to escort Sana back to the dormitory, and she waited, bracing herself for his inevitable retaliation. However, days passed without any indication of his anger. Initially, she remained tense, fearing the worst with each creak of the door. But over time, she resigned herself to accept whatever fate lay in store and ceased feeling apprehensive.

More than two weeks elapsed without Saeed summoning her. Nevertheless, in the third week, he called upon her once more.

# Chapter Fourteen
# Mother's Prayers and Father's Pleas

Sana made her way into Lieutenant Colonel Saeed's office, and he gestured for her to take a seat. A cup of coffee was placed in front of her, but she took only a small sip, too lost in thought to enjoy the taste. She couldn't fathom how she had managed to survive thus far, and she couldn't help but wonder what Saeed intended to do with her. She remained silent, waiting for the worst to come.

"Sana, I have some news for you," Saeed said, breaking the silence.

She braced herself for the worst, imagining that he was going to subject her to torture instead of execution.

"There is no easy way to say this, so I'll just come out with it. I received word from sources within the army that during a raid on terrorist sites in Eastern Ghouta, your parents were among the people who were killed."

Sana's face drained of all color, her pupils dilated, and she shivered uncontrollably. She tried to speak, but no words came out. Her heart raced so fast she thought it would burst. Sweat dripped from every pore on her body, and she collapsed onto the floor, unconscious.

When Sana came to, she found herself in the dormitory surrounded by the other women. She struggled to make sense of what had happened, hoping that it was all just a terrible nightmare. She thought about her parents, their prayers, and her father's pleas. She shut her eyes, hoping that when she opened them again, she would wake up to find that it had all been a terrible fever dream.

The days that followed were a blur for Sana. She struggled to separate reality from fantasy, unable to tell whether she was alive or dead. Even the unspeakable torture she had been subjected to didn't affect her as much as this. Umm Abboud, her caretaker, did her best to comfort Sana, stroking her hair, calming her nerves, and encouraging her to eat and drink. The children in the dormitory gathered around their exhausted teacher, offering her their support, reciting the prepositions and numbers she had taught them, but Sana's mind was elsewhere. The truth was just too much to bear, and she found herself clinging to her imaginary world, where dreams and imagination illuminated the darkness and restored balance to her life.

As Sana recalled Umm Abboud's poignant words, her heart ached with a deep sense of loss. She couldn't help but ponder over the sorry state of affairs in her country—a nation ravaged by the greed and lust for power of its rulers. Her people had lost everything—their patriotism, sense of belonging, pride, and honor. Her homeland was now a victim of relentless exploitation, stripped bare of its dignity and self-respect.

Umm Abboud's words had struck a chord within her, and Sana felt an overwhelming urge to escape this wretched world. She knew it was time to bid farewell to all that was dear to her and leave without looking back. Her soul was weary, and the thought of living in such a brutal and tragic world made her heart heavy.

However, even as Sana contemplated surrender, she couldn't shake off the words of Mansour, her parents, and Dr. Imad. Each of them reminded her that surrendering meant losing, that she couldn't give up, and that it would render her life meaningless.

Thus, as Umm Abboud's words continued to echo in her mind, Sana struggled to come back to reality. She knew that giving up wasn't an option and that she had to fight for what was right. With a newfound sense of purpose, Sana resolved to stay and fight until the bitter end.

*Returning to life felt like an existential war, a battle that I wasn't sure I was ready to fight. Death, in comparison, seemed like a peaceful escape from the brutality and injustice that I, and countless others, had suffered. For a time, it felt as though surrender was the only option, and I was tempted to leave without a word of farewell.*

*But as I thought, I knew that I couldn't give in so easily. The pain and suffering that I had endured, the crimes that had been committed against me and my people, could not be ignored or forgotten. Those who were responsible for such cruelty and injustice had to be punished, and my continued existence was the first step toward that end.*

*It was a difficult decision to choose life over death, but I knew that it was the right one. I had to keep fighting, to keep living, even when it seemed like the world was against me. The road ahead would be long and challenging, but I was determined to see it through. The thought of justice, of finally finding some measure of peace, gave me the strength to carry on.*

Despite feeling weak and weighed down, Sana understood that she needed to take charge of her own recovery. Though those around her were eager to assist, they were unsure of how to do so. It was up to Sana to summon the strength within herself and forge a path back to reality.

## Chapter Fifteen
## Al Mabouja

Sana received a summons from Lieutenant Colonel Saeed. He greeted her with a hidden smile and spoke to her in a friendly tone, "Sana, there is going to be an exchange of prisoners, and you will be among those who will be released." She was unsure about who put her name on the list, but the prospect of finally leaving the prison filled her with hope.

The women in the dormitory celebrated her release and extended their greetings to her family and friends. Umm, Abboud hugged her tightly, shedding tears of joy, and encouraged her to take care of herself and keep moving forward. Her belongings were distributed among her fellow prisoners, and she left the facility with only the clothes she wore and the list of heroines.

The exchange was scheduled to take place in the town of Al-Saan in the eastern countryside of Hama. Sana joined a group of sixteen others, including ten women, on the bus that departed at eight in the morning. Still early, most of the shops in the capital were closed. The streets were adorned with pictures of the current president's father, Hasan Nasrallah, Vladimir Putin, and Qassem Suleimani. Hezbollah flags and other flags unfamiliar to Sana were raised at every checkpoint. The usual shabiha slogans were painted on the walls, such as 'Assad or we burn the country,' 'Assad forever,' and 'Assad's Syria.'

During the journey, the bus stopped several times at checkpoints, where shabiha carrying guns cheered for the homeland's leader, cursed the terrorists on the bus, and threatened them. They even spat on them, raised their middle fingers, and shouted that they would track them down no matter where they went.

The bus ride from Damascus to Al-Saan took more than eighteen hours, mostly due to frequent checkpoints in Homs and Al-Salamiyah. Eventually, the exchange took place in Al-Saan, where twenty-five regime forces members were swapped for Sana and her fellow detainees. Upon their arrival in Hama, the townspeople welcomed them with food, water, and cheers, demanding the release of all prisoners and the overthrow of the regime. They also issued threats against the culprits.

One of the recipients was Sana's aunt, Wafa, who had requested her niece's name to be added to the exchange list. Wafa took Sana to her home in the small village of Al-Mabuja, located in the eastern countryside of Hama. Despite the presence of checkpoints, Wafa's husband, Sarmad, who was of the Ismaili[9] sect facilitated their passage without any inspections.

In Syria, inter-sect marriages were not necessarily uncommon, but they did not receive broad acceptance. Wafa and Sarmad's union had faced such opposition. Al-Mabuja is a diverse village with a population of Sunnis, Ismailis, and Alawites. Sarmad and Wafa met while studying at the Faculty of Law in Damascus, and they decided to marry despite their families' objections. They settled in Sarmad's hometown of Al-

---

[9] Isma'ilism is a branch or sect of Shia Islam. The Isma'ili (/ˌɪsmeɪˈɪli/) get their name from their acceptance of Imam Isma'il ibn Jafar as the appointed spiritual successor (imām) to Ja'far al-Sadiq, wherein they differ from the Twelver Shia, who accept Musa al-Kadhim, the younger brother of Isma'il, as the true Imām. The Shia Ismailis form the largest branch of Shia Islam in Syria, forming three percent **of Syria's population.**

Mabuja, where they were initially boycotted, but their situation improved over time, particularly after they had their daughter, Dima.

During the exchange process from Al-Saan to Al-Mabuja, Wafa attempted to converse with Sana, who didn't speak. The car ride was silent, made even quieter by the brief ceasefire between the warring factions.

Sana yearned to rest. Upon entering the house, she made her way to her cousin Dima's room, which she knew well from their childhood playtimes. The room appeared exactly as Sana remembered it, with purple still the dominant color. Although Dima had gotten married and immigrated to Canada years ago, her belongings remained unchanged. Sana spotted a picture of them together in a wooden frame on the shelf, and there was a small library in the corner with a few books, a chair, and a table. Dolls were scattered about the room. She fell into a deep slumber.

*The situation felt so surreal. The days of facing jailers, torture, insults, and degradation were long gone. Now, all that remained was silence, occasionally interrupted by the distant sound of music. I couldn't help but wonder, could this be the end? Had my endless suffering finally come to an end?*

Sana retreated into her room for days, unable to face the world beyond the four walls surrounding her. Her body had wasted away, leaving her looking like a sickly, yellowed specter with bulging eyes. She barely ate, surviving on mere crumbs. It wasn't the relief of being released from prison that left her in such a state, but a deep, gnawing pain that consumed her. She groaned and wept, her sorrow a palpable thing that left Wafaa and Sarmad feeling helpless in their attempts to comfort her.

After some time, they called in a doctor who confirmed several of Sana's broken bones had healed poorly, particularly in her hands and ribcage. The doctor prescribed painkillers, sedatives, and other medications to address the infections, scabies, and inflammation that had taken hold of her body. But the medication only left her in a haze of sleep and excruciating pain, waking up in the middle of the night with screams that shook the walls of the house. In her agony, Wafaa held her close and wept with her, knowing that there was little she could do to ease her niece's suffering.

During her time in detention, Sana had learned to cope with the physical pain of torture, beatings, and broken bones. But now, her pain was primarily psychological. She grieved for the women and children left behind in prison, as well as Umm Abboud and her parents, who she was separated from without the chance to say goodbye. Thoughts of Mansour and her country's dire situation that surrounded her tormented her every waking moment.

It took more than a month for Sana to come to terms with her new reality.

# Chapter Sixteen
# Clothes of Decency and Modesty

Sana preferred to avoid public places in Al-Mabouja for her family's safety. The village was tense, with different sects and affiliations drawing lines in the sand. Sunnis backed the opposition, while Alawites supported the regime. Ismailis were divided, and extremism had even seeped into the community that once prided itself on coexistence. Sarmad had warned her about the current state of affairs, describing it as paranoid. The loyalists viewed the opposition as extremists, while the opposition saw the loyalists as slaves of a criminal dictator. The neutrals[10] were apathetic and just wished for things to return to how they were before.

Despite her best efforts, news of Sana's presence in the village spread like wildfire. Fearing that her stay might cause trouble for her relatives, Sana decided to flee to Idlib. Unfortunately, fate had other plans.

On the day she was to depart, ISIS descended upon the village in a violent attack, causing widespread destruction and chaos. Over fifty civilians were killed, and many more were

---

[10] Syrians who do not consider themselves Assad loyalists, but there is often a sense of political apathy or lack of belief that a different society could be possible. Such Syrians frequently describe themselves as politically "neutral" or "grey" (ramady) and focus instead on personal material success and stability. Many so-called neutrals as well as loyalists tend to look back with nostalgia on the era of relative social order and the submersion of sectarian and ethnic differences that was enforced under the Baathist dictatorship.

injured or kidnapped. Sana found herself among the ten kidnapped civilians, blindfolded, and shoved into a Toyota truck. The members of ISIS were jubilant, chanting 'Allah is the Greatest' and firing shots into the air to celebrate their success. Stories about ISIS prisoners were well-known, with captives sold, executed, or forced to marry fighters from the group.

Sana and the other kidnapped women arrived in Raqqa, exhausted and shaken. They were separated from the men and taken to a foreboding underground prison. A member of the Hisba[11], one of the organization's enforcers coldly informed them that they were to be sold in the market the following day. The women were left to worry, filled with dread and hopelessness.

As the evening descended, the Hisba women made their way to the seven abducted women. They gave them food and a new set of clothes, black galabias[12] and niqabs to befit the expectations of decency and modesty. The women proceeded to inquire about each woman's background, age, religion, and, most importantly, their virginity status. The answers to these questions would hold great value in determining their worth in the market the next day.

---

[11] The Hisba of ISIS is a well-known security agency with significant influence and authority, second only to the organization's intelligence agency, which is responsible for regulating civilian life, including monitoring prayer times and holding shopkeepers accountable for closing during them. There is a women's office that intervenes if women have a problem or issue, as well as applying hudud* on women and searching their homes. The Hisba roamed the streets of Raqqa and ensured women dressed appropriately.

[12] Traditional robes worn by both men and women, usually in the Middle East.

# Chapter Seventeen
# Al Rasheed Park

The next morning, the seven women were led in handcuffs to Al-Rasheed Park in the heart of Raqqa. Once a place for families and children to revel in picnics and entertainment, the park had been transformed into a slave market. Sana looked around in horror as she surveyed the once beautiful garden, now reduced to ruins. Overturned chairs and broken children's toys lay scattered around. The few trees that remained were either uprooted, burnt, or cut down. Despite it being spring, there were no flowers in sight. Instead, a canopy of wood had been erected in the center of the park.

The crowd of civilians had fear in their eyes. Women dressed in galabias hid their faces behind their niqabs, while men in Afghan clothes kept their gaze lowered—whether out of shyness or fear, Sana couldn't say. The children's demeanor matched the dark clothes they were dressed in. Everyone was compelled to attend the auction.

Members of the organization, dressed in a shalwar, which appeared to be Afghan, and wielding rifles, shouted orders at the civilians to line up for the slave market. They used physical violence and verbal abuse to force the people to comply. The Hisba women, armed with long sticks and hurling insults, compelled other women to join the auction as well. Children between the ages of ten and fifteen, dressed in military uniforms and carrying weapons, stood silently, wearing badges on their chests with the inscription 'The Cubs of the Caliphate.' They awaited the orders of their commander.

The seven women, including Sana, were lined up on the platform, dressed in black with only their eyes visible and their hands and feet bound with iron chains. A large ISIS fighter with a red beard and an Arab headdress stood next to them, brandishing a gun and scanning the crowd with anger and disgust. He raised his hand, and everyone fell silent, including the children.

The auction began, and the fighter began describing the women's characteristics, including their ages, origins, and educational backgrounds. He also mentioned whether they were virgins, categorizing them as suitable for marriage, concubinage, or servitude. The auction continued, and the six other women were sold to fighters from the organization. Sana remained on the platform as the final woman to be sold in the ISIS market. Her mind was blank, and she felt numb—perhaps a defense mechanism to shield herself from panic and terror, to protect herself from her own emotions and from what would come next.

*How did human life become so cheap? What had happened to this world, where women were sold in auctions and turned into concubines and slave girls, and men became chained slaves, and children became fighters, carrying weapons instead of playing, learning, laughing, and having fun? The questions weighed heavily on Sana's mind as she stood on the platform.*

Surrounded by a throng of armed guards, a man stood at the center of the bustling crowd, his hand raised in command from atop the podium. Sana was then taken to a nearby house, escorted inside, and left alone with a single guard. She sat and waited, her eyes fixed on the door, anticipating the arrival of Abu Omar.

The house consisted of only two rooms: a bedroom with only a bed and wardrobe, without any personal effects or clothing, and a dusty living room with well-worn sofas and a table made of antique wood. The kitchen was small and basic, equipped with only a gas stove, a refrigerator, and some old utensils. Moss had begun to grow in the corners, further evidence of neglect and decay.

As she sat in the dimly lit room, Sana felt the weight of her situation bear down on her. The squalor of her surroundings only served to deepen her sense of despair and hopelessness.

*Once again, my path has led me to a life filled with pain, humiliation, heartbreak, and anguish. I find myself caught between the al-Khatib branch in Damascus, the solitary cell, and the wet dormitory where I endured torture, beatings, and rape. And now, I am in the house of the infamous 'Samarrai' in Raqqa, a worn-out place that reeks of death and destruction. Despite the hundreds of kilometers between these places, my destiny is marred by humiliation, judgments, immoral practices, and sequences of guardianship. I am left wondering what the end of this journey will be, unsure of how to survive and continue living in the face of such adversity.*

# Chapter Eighteen
# Al-Samarrai

The infamous Al-Samarrai was a prominent figure in ISIS, known for his brutal and tyrannical ways. He was short and round, in his forties, and had held various positions within the organization. Considered to be one of the close associates of the leader of ISIS, Abu Bakr al-Baghdadi, he had a reputation for his past filled with crime. He had been responsible for a training camp in Iraq and later became a commander of operations in the state of Raqqa[13]. His legacy was marked by the execution of hundreds of civilians and military personnel during battles in Iraq and Syria.

Al-Samarrai was constantly present on the front lines in Raqqa, but he no longer led battles. Instead, he directed the commanders and lectured them to benefit from his knowledge and experience. He toured the front lines frequently to meet with fighters and to offer support. His speeches centered on jihad and martyrdom for the sake of God, and he promised the establishment of an Islamic state in all Muslim countries, often talking about paradise and the nymphs. He even distributed money to fighters to gain their loyalty and incited them to kill, take captives, and seize spoils. With verses and hadiths taken out of context, he often ended his resonant sermons with the phrase 'Death to the infidels.'

---

[13] Raqqa served as the de-facto capital of the Islamic State between January 2014–October 2017

In his youth, Al-Samarrai had been a drunkard who frequented nightclubs in Tikrit, Iraq. He spent his nights with dancers and prostitutes, wandering the city streets with a knife, searching for food or money to spend on a night of drunken orgies, which he called 'a red night.' He was imprisoned multiple times, but he always returned back to his old ways upon release. However, after spending over twenty years in this drunken limbo, he was imprisoned once again and met Islamist individuals who convinced him to convert to Islam. Upon his release, he joined ISIS, becoming a sheik who wielded arms to maim people, replacing his previous method of using a knife.

Despite joining ISIS, Al-Samarrai continued to drink, but he became better at hiding it. He also became skilled at systematic armed robbery and purchasing women for sexual pleasure, seizing several houses in Raqqa that belonged to prominent families. Using force, he expelled the owners and confiscated their belongings, claiming it was for the Caliphate and Islam. He established these houses as military bases and homes for his harem, consisting of wives and many concubines whom he referred to as 'to whom your right hands possess[14].' To avoid being targeted by the international coalition against ISIS, Al-Samarrai changed houses frequently and never slept in the same place for more than two consecutive nights.

By chance, Al-Samarrai chose Sana as his new concubine in the auction. He had been touring the fronts and arrived late to an auction after delivering a long sermon about heaven, rivers of wine, and al-hoor al-'in[15]. All six women had already been sold,

---

[14] From a phrase in the Quran, "to whom your right hands possess" usually refers to women taken as prisoners of war. Many would argue that ISIS were applying the phrase to an extreme by purchasing women from markets to satisfy their sexual urges.

[15] In Islam, al-hoor al-'in are women with beautiful eyes who are described as a reward for the faithful Muslim men in paradise.

but he declared that God had sent him a new concubine as his share.

He took her to a house that he had recently occupied, which had previously been inhabited by a woman in her sixties. He threw the previous occupant out in the street and triumphantly entered the house in the name of religion. He chose this particular house because it overlooked Saif al-Dawla Street, one of the city's most significant streets, with windows exposed on three sides, allowing him to see everything around him. The house was located on the third floor of a five-story building where dozens of civilians also lived. This made it difficult and costly for American drones to target, as they had become a frequent tool in hunting down leaders of the organization. In the event that the house's location was discovered by coalition forces, they would not risk killing dozens of civilians to eliminate it.

He ordered one of his wives to supervise the cleaning and preparation of the house, and he instructed her to place women's clothes inside. He also had one of his trusted men smuggle bottles of whiskey and beer into the house before his arrival.

Before purchasing Sana, Al-Samarrai committed one of the most brutal acts when he bought a Yazidi woman and her daughter, transported them to Raqqa, and subjected them to all forms of persecution, including starvation. He even punished the five-year-old girl for wetting her bed by tying her to the window handle of the house. With a temperature of over forty degrees Celsius, the girl died of thirst. He forced the mother to go out into the street barefoot, almost naked and burned her alive. It's important to note that ISIS considered the Yazidis infidels and killed large numbers of them in the Sinjar district of Nineveh Governorate, their stronghold in Iraq. Tens of thousands of Yazidis were forced to flee, and ISIS detained girls and women, exploiting them sexually and transferring many to Syria.

# Chapter Nineteen
# If You Stare Too Long Into the Abyss

Sana found herself trapped in the house once again, her future uncertain. She sat in silence, feeling helpless and alone, as a flood of questions raced through her mind. Would she be forced to serve as a maid or a slave woman? Would she have to endure the horrific scenes of rape and torture she had witnessed before? Was her life an endless cycle of pain and suffering? Was suicide her only escape from this nightmare?

Before Sana could escape her troubled thoughts, al-Samarrai barged into the house, grabbing her by the hand and dragging her into the bedroom. He ripped off her black robe and flung her onto the bed, attempting to force himself upon her. However, Sana refused to submit, fighting him off with all her strength. She kicked, hit, and even bit him, screaming and resisting his advances. Eventually, she managed to break free and ran into the bathroom, locking the door behind her.

But al-Samarrai was not deterred. He broke down the bathroom door, dragging Sana out by her hair and throwing her to the ground. Despite her attempts to fight back, he overpowered her, hitting her and throwing her back onto the bed like a savage beast. Sana huddled in a corner of the bed, refusing to let him attempt to rape her again. She would rather die than suffer such a tragedy once more.

Though Sana remained silent, her unspoken words were clear to al-Samarrai. Her silence only provoked him further, and he began to beat her mercilessly. She groaned and screamed in agony, her blood spilling onto the sheets. Finally, he left her lying in a pool of her own blood, alone and broken.

Sana remained in bed, unconscious and in pain, until the morning after al-Samarrai had left. When she awoke, she found a kind woman wiping the blood from her face. The woman introduced herself as Umm Ali, a neighbor in the building, and explained that the guard had asked her to care for Sana. Umm Ali helped Sana to the bathroom, where she cleaned her up, changed her clothes, and combed her hair.

During their conversation, Umm Ali recounted tales of al-Samarrai's past actions, including the one involving the Yazidi woman and her daughter. Umm Ali, a widowed woman in her fifties, had been left alone after her children were forced out of the city due to the arrival of ISIS. She depended on her nephew, who came to visit her once a week to provide her with any necessities.

When ISIS took control of the city, Umm Ali's husband was still alive. However, ISIS fighters demanded that he spy on the people in their neighborhood. He refused, and as a result, they detained him for ten days. He tried to escape, but they shot and killed him, and his body was later sent to her.

Several days later, a group of four young ISIS fighters arrived at the woman's house and occupied it for a week. They confined her to one room where she could hear them bring in a new girl each day. The girls were taken to the next room, where the fighters would take turns raping them for hours. Most of the girls were under the age of fifteen, and the woman could hear their cries and screams through the common wall between the two rooms.

When she tried to object, one of the fighters struck her on

the head with the butt of a gun and threatened her with death. After a week, they abandoned the house and moved to another location, leaving Umm Ali behind.

Umm Ali had been left alone by the ISIS fighters who had occupied her house for a week before moving on to their next location, leaving behind a trail of destruction and fear.

After witnessing the atrocities committed against the women in her community, Umm Ali was determined to help in any way she could. "I vowed to help the girls in this area," she said to Sana, anger and determination etched on her face. "The treatment of women under ISIS is appalling. They're treated like property and have no rights."

Umm Ali recounted the restrictions and control that ISIS had placed upon women, forbidding them from working in most fields and limiting them to roles like nursing or selling women's clothing. Marriage was also controlled by ISIS, with fighters able to choose any woman they desired, even going so far as to specify in their will that their wife must marry a man of their choosing. Women were forced to wear black clothing and forbidden from raising their voices in the presence of men.

Despite the dangers, Sana and Umm Ali had become close friends and spent most of their time together. But the absence of al-Samarrai had not gone unnoticed. He had not visited the house in over a month, and his threatening messages through his assistants had only intensified. Sana confided in Umm Ali about her plan to deal with him, and with her help, she hoped to succeed.

"If you're planning to escape," warned Umm Ali. "You need to be extremely cautious. Al-Samarrai and his fighters are ruthless." She recounted the story of the fifty women from the village of Hawija Halawa who were detained, abused, and brutally killed. Another story she heard was about Fathia, a woman who suffered unimaginable horror at the hands of al-Samarrai and his men.

Nonetheless, Sana was determined to proceed. "My plan is solid," she said to Umm Ali. "But I need to figure out how to avoid him when he comes home. Can you help me with that?" Umm Ali hesitated, knowing the danger of going up against someone like al-Samarrai, but eventually agreed after hearing Sana's pleas.

*I can't help but notice that all of these groups—ISIS, the regime, the militias—they're all the same, they're all fighting for their own interests, serving an ugly dictatorship and upholding authoritarianism, often using religion, nationalism, race or sect as a cover. They prey on the vulnerable, taking everything from them, humiliating them, and stealing from them. But they don't realize that the weak can one day become fierce predators, seeking retribution for all the harm they've caused. I just stared too long into the abyss.*

# Chapter Twenty
# Award for Best Actress

"Send someone to prepare her for my visit tonight," Al-Samarrai instructed one of his men.

Sana tried reaching out to people in the city through Umm Ali, though she didn't fully trust any of them. She knew resisting Al-Samarrai was not a viable strategy, so that evening, she prepared herself for his visit.

Sana chose to wear one of the revealing dresses left in the closet: a low-cut, sleeveless red dress cut just above the knee. She tied her hair back, put on some makeup, found a bottle of whiskey in the house, and prepared some appetizers using the limited ingredients she had on hand.

When Al-Samarrai arrived, he left his weapons with the guards at the door. Sana greeted him with a smile and led him into the living room. As they sat together, Sana poured him a glass of whiskey, which he drank quickly. She poured him a second glass, which he also finished promptly. He then grabbed the bottle and poured himself more, eventually finishing it all.

*He drinks like a camel,* Sana thought to herself.

Al-Samarrai began eating the food Sana had prepared, devouring everything on the table. *He eats like an elephant,* she thought to herself. All of her thoughts at the time were related to animals—bears, camels, elephants—perhaps reflecting her belief that Al-Samarrai was driven solely by his animal instincts.

"I'll get another bottle," she said with a wink and a smile.

She entered the kitchen and retrieved another bottle of whiskey, which she opened and proceeded to pour the sleeping pills concoction that Umm Ali had provided her.

Upon returning to the living room, she poured him a new glass and watched as he began to lose consciousness. She smiled, took his hand, and led him to the bedroom.

Once in the bedroom, he lay on the bed waiting for her, and she asked his permission to go to the bathroom to prepare herself. She stayed in the bathroom for over half an hour, giving him enough time to sleep deeply. When she emerged, he was snoring heavily and appeared completely unconscious.

Sana imagined him as a sleeping buffalo as his chest rose and fell. Although she thought, *I could kill him;* she knew that doing so would mean the end of her life. She was trapped, with his men stationed outside the door. Even if she could escape them, she would not be able to evade the Hisba in the street. Instead, she needed to find a safe and effective way to escape.

She stripped al-Samarrai of his lower clothes and laid naked next to him. She wanted to convince him that he had taken what he wanted from her and that he was satisfied. She did not sleep that night, pretending to be asleep, hoping that her plan would succeed.

In the morning, al-Samarrai woke up half-naked with clothes scattered everywhere. He was proud of himself. He went to the bathroom, and she quickly put her clothes back on, waiting for him to return. When he did, he was ready to leave, but Sana stopped him before he reached the door:

"Abu Omar, can I go to the market to buy some things?" she asked, looking at him.

He nodded. "I will tell the guard to accompany you whenever you want to the market; take this money; it will suffice until my next visit."

As he was about to leave, she stopped him again, using all her energy to convince him that she wanted to see him again so that he would not suspect anything.

"When will I see you again?" she asked, her voice trembling with anxiety.

She wanted to know how long she had to find a way out of this place.

"Depends, in two to three weeks," he replied and then left.

Sana breathed a sigh of relief as she watched him go, grateful that her plan had succeeded. She needed to find a way out quickly to escape from this place. But for now, she was safe, and that was all that mattered.

*Mastering the role was not a simple task. It involved more than just persuading others. I had to fully embody and internalize the character, burying any feelings of hatred, disgust, or distress that might surface. I had to conceal any resentment or negative emotions, ensuring that they did not affect my actions, words, or movements. Every detail had to be perfect; failure was not an option. Winning the award for best actress was crucial, as anything less would be a disaster. That night, I exhausted all of my energy. It felt like I was in a scene from an absurd play by Eugene Ionesco or Samuel Beckett. When he finally left, it was like the closing of the curtain, marking the end of that chapter.*

# Chapter Twenty-One
# Cigarettes Kill, and So Do We

Sana and Umm Ali emerged from the building onto 23 February Street, a bustling thoroughfare in Raqqa that ran from the ancient wall and industrial zone in the east to Al-Rasheed Park in the west. The young man tasked by al-Samarrai to escort and watch over Sana walked behind them as they turned onto Al Mujamma Street toward the Armenian Church. Several young men dressed in what appeared to be Afghan clothes and armed with weapons stood guard outside the entrance.

This was the first time Sana traveled through areas controlled by ISIS. As they walked, a sign along the road caught her eye—a picture of a cigarette spewing blood with the warning 'Cigarettes Kill.' Another sign read 'My Hijab, My Pride' in bold letters with 'Your Brothers from the Sharia'a Office' written in small print underneath. Yet another sign listed the strict conditions for a woman to leave her house wearing a legally acceptable hijab. The walls were covered in menacing phrases and threats, urging residents to comply with Islamic law.

The city was shrouded in darkness, and a sense of despair hung in the air. Men looked back at the past with sadness, while women's faces were covered in black, hiding their buried nostalgia. ISIS members roamed the neighborhoods, intimidating and threatening civilians while searching shops. The women's militia carried sticks, beating women and directing them as they pleased. The city felt like a prison, with powerless detainees who remained out of inability to escape, not out of love. They followed orders out of fear, not conviction.

During an inspection tour of a school, the Al-Khansaa Brigade arrested ten female students wearing niqabs—for putting on makeup under the veil—claiming they were illegal. The girls were flogged as punishment. In addition, the battalion arrested three other girls in the city center who had removed their niqabs. The girls were sentenced to thirty lashes each by an ISIS judge.

Cages lined with skulls were placed throughout the city and carefully positioned near cemeteries or public squares. Young men and women were trapped inside as punishment for violating the regulations.

As Sana looked around, she felt a deep sense of sadness for the people who lived there. The city had become a shadow of its former self, with its inhabitants living in constant fear. Here, life became a struggle for survival.

Each cage in the city bore a statement of punishment that had been approved by one of the organization's judges and had been read by the organization's shari'a during execution. Sana observed as they walked through the streets. Sana shuddered at the thought of being trapped inside one of them.

The punishment for those confined in the cages varied, ranging from hours to days. Sana heard stories from other women during her capture under Samarrai of a fifteen-year-old girl placed in a cage for a full day for not wearing her veil correctly, a young man in his twenties confined for three days for failing to pray, and another sentenced to hundred lashes and a week in a cage for being caught with cigarettes. A woman in her forties was sentenced to two days in a cage for raising her voice in front of one of the Hisba women, and a man in his fifties for two days for refusing to marry his daughter off to an ISIS fighter. The punishment was brutal, and some of those confined to the cages suffered from mental breakdowns or committed suicide.

Sana and Umm Ali eventually arrived in front of a shop covered with curtains. "This is the place I told you about, Sana," said Umm Ali.

Sana asked why there wasn't anything in the window, to which Umm Ali explained, "Women's clothing is forbidden to be placed on the front, and even the seller must be a woman."

A young man followed them, tasked with watching over Sana. Umm Ali spoke to him, "This is a women's clothing store. You can't go in."

The young man examined the place, knocked on the door, and a veiled woman came out, allowing them to enter. The woman was happy to see Umm Ali and asked her about her news, acquaintances, and friends. She helped Sana pick out some underwear and gave it to her.

"Go into the changing room; you have to be quick; the Hisba patrols come without an appointment," Umm Ali instructed Sana.

Sana entered the small room covered with a brown curtain, where there was a large mirror on the wall and a small hook on the left for hanging clothes. After hanging her small bag and veil, Sana waited for a few minutes. Suddenly, the wall on which the mirror was located opened, revealing a young girl no more than twelve years old, who motioned for Sana to go to the next room.

In the empty room, Sana sat on a wooden chair in the corner and waited for Al-Hawari, the man whom Umm Ali had arranged to help her escape the city. She heard footsteps approaching, and soon enough, the door opened, and Al-Hawari entered. He was a young man in his thirties, wearing a white galabia and a red headscarf. He greeted Sana with a light smile that comforted her.

"Peace be upon you, my dear," greeted al-Hawari as he introduced himself to Sana. "Umm Ali told me about you. God willing, I will help you get out of the city."

Sana expressed her concerns about not having anything to offer him in exchange for his help, but al-Hawari reassured her. "Don't worry, my sister. I don't want anything from you. The important thing is that you get out safely with the help of God Almighty. You are from Damascus, and it is very dear to us."

Sana had been told about al-Hawari's background and how he used his clan connections to help families escape from ISIS oppression. Al-Hawari informed Sana that he was planning to smuggle a family of six out of the city and that she could go with them. "I promise to send the exact date through Umm Ali," he said.

Their conversation was interrupted by the flashing of the ceiling light, signaling the arrival of a Hisba patrol. Al-Hawari instructed Sana to go back to the changing room and promised to inform her of the time soon.

Sana's heart raced as she reentered the changing room, where she could hear muffled voices from outside. She called out from behind the curtain, pretending to be in the middle of a transaction. A woman entered, and Sana recognized her as one of the Hisba due to the stick in her hand. The woman slapped Sana forcefully in the face and started searching her while beating her with sticks on her feet, buttocks, and chest.

Umm Ali intervened, explaining that Sana belonged to the Samarrai and was there to buy suitable clothes for her man. The Hisba woman stopped and examined Sana with a piercing look. "Samarrai's woman, okay, that's why there's an officer out there with you," she said.

Sana paid for the clothes and left the shop with Umm Ali, walking toward the house without exchanging any words.

## Chapter Twenty-Two
## Mixed Feelings

Sana received the news four days later. She was instructed to leave the city that very evening and to meet a man in the alley behind the building at exactly nine o'clock. The man would be carrying a black bag and wearing a black scarf, and to confirm his identity, she must ask for his name. If he replied with the code word 'Al-Zarqawi,' then she would know he was the real deal. Time was of the essence, and punctuality was emphasized.

During the past four days, Sana had developed a rapport with the guard who was stationed at her door. Each day, she would serve him dinner at six o'clock, insisting that he needed the sustenance more than the meals provided by al-Sammerai's crew. On the fourth day, she added a sedative to his meal, hoping to incapacitate him. However, when he thanked her for the meal, he claimed to have already eaten and promised to eat it later. As the clock neared eight, and he still hadn't touched his food, Sana knew she had to act fast. She made a glass of orange juice, added the sedative, and used extra sugar to mask the flavor.

Sana reminded herself of the clear instructions, taking nothing with her except her handbag. She wore only the clothes on her back and the lingerie she had purchased from Al-Hawari's shop, along with the money that had been given to her by al-Samarrai and Umm Ali. She took a knife from the kitchen, making sure the guard drank the juice before leaving at exactly nine o'clock to meet al-Zarqawi behind the building.

After waiting for a few tense moments, a breathless al-

Zarqawi arrived, urging Sana to hurry as there was a patrol nearby. Sana hesitated, noticing that he wasn't carrying a black bag or wearing a black scarf. She quickly pushed him away when he tried to grab her hand.

"Who are you?" she demanded.

"I am Al-Zarqawi," he panted. "During my escape from the patrol, I had to throw my bag and lose my scarf while running."

"Who sent you?" she pressed.

"Al-Hawari."

Sana was still hesitant but knew going home wasn't an option with a guard lying on the ground and al-Samarrai returning soon. She had no other choice but to continue.

Together, Sana and al-Zarqawi moved cautiously through the alleys, weaving through demolished buildings and taking side roads to evade Hisbah patrols. They eventually reached the outskirts of the city, where they met the Abu Mahmoud family and the first vehicle that would take them on their journey. Al-Hawari said his goodbyes, wishing them success in leaving the ISIS-controlled areas. Al-Zarqawi would be Sana's escort for the journey.

The journey from Raqqa to Aleppo typically takes only two hours, but their travels required parts by bus and parts by foot and ended up taking eight days and nights. They had to walk long distances, sometimes more than twenty kilometers at night, to reach the next bus. They huddled together to stave off the desert cold. They had to expand their circle several times to avoid detection and outflank ISIS.

At times, the roar of planes overhead and the bombing of ISIS positions forced them to lie on the ground, even near the battlefronts, atop thorns that cut them and drew blood from their hands and feet.

Sana's heart was torn in two as she grappled with her conflicting emotions. On the one hand, her desire for the utter annihilation of the ISIS hideouts, particularly the menacing al-Samarrai and his accomplices, consumed her thoughts. But on the other hand, she could not shake off the haunting image of the innocent civilians who called those areas home, like Umm Ali and al-Hawari. The sheer weight of this heartbreaking dilemma weighed heavily on Sana's soul.

After eight long days and nights, they finally arrived at the outskirts of Azaz in northern Aleppo, which was under the control of the armed opposition. The last vehicle that brought them there left, and Al-Zarqawi informed them that he couldn't take them any further. They had to walk the rest of the way to reach the city center, which took them several hours.

Luckily, their smuggler didn't abandon them, and Al-Hawari covered all the expenses of the trip, which would have cost thousands of dollars. Al-Zarqawi instructed the smuggler not to leave them until they reached safety, which they finally found on the outskirts of Azaz.

*The journey to Azaz was a challenging one. The physical fatigue was bearable; I had grown accustomed to the long walks and harsh conditions. What weighed heavily on me were the thoughts of hundreds of thousands of civilians trapped in that dark and dismal place, with their hearts and souls tainted by the ugliness of it all.*

*Living in that big prison was too disheartening to put into words. I couldn't help but wonder, is this the fate of all Syrians now? To be at the mercy of a criminal nationalist dictatorship on one side and a murderous religious terrorist organization on the other? Are we destined to endure endless raids, bombings, death, arrests, torture, and rape? Has our dignity and humanity become so worthless to these tyrants?*

# Chapter Twenty-Three
# Dreams

Ten years prior, Sana had accompanied her mother and her mother's friends to Azaz, a city located near the Turkish border, to shop for smuggled luxury Turkish goods. During that time, conservative, middle-class women would purchase long skirts and white ornate veils from Azaz. However, things have taken a turn for the worse since then. This time around, the visit felt more like that of a displaced person trying to survive rather than a shopper looking for a sale.

Once they had arrived in the main square, everyone stood exhausted and relieved, exchanging worried glances with a sense of disbelief. Some exhibited signs of relief, yet their emotions were mixed with heartbreak and fear of the unknown. Sana feigned being busy, rummaging through her bag until the conversation ended. As Abu Mahmoud and his wife left the main square with their family, Sana remained rooted to her spot, unsure of what to do next. The only question that echoed in her mind was, *What now?* Fatigue crept into her bones, and all she yearned for was sleep. With limited options available, she chose a hidden corner in a nearby public park where she could rest her exhausted body on the ground and fall asleep.

Over the years, Sana's body had developed several defense mechanisms, including the ability to bear pain, adapt to her surroundings, and require minimal food, among others. However, the most significant defense mechanism that her body had developed was the ability to block dreams or nightmares, except for a few exceptions. Despite all the tragedies she had endured, her body had denied her dreams to safeguard her from nightmares and provide her with the rest she needed to survive.

But that night, Sana's dreams returned. She found herself transported back in time to the moment she first met Mansour at the Opera House and to happy moments spent with her parent's friends and during her university days. It was as though her body was trying to bring back some joy to her memories and remind her of what life could have been like if things had taken a different turn. However, the reality of everything she had endured quickly dawned on her, and she realized that everything that had happened to her was not just a dream but a harsh reality.

Sana's first priority was to find shelter. Renting a house in the city was not financially feasible for her at the moment, as the money she had brought from Raqqa would only cover one month's rent. She decided to save the money for emergencies or for food if she couldn't find a job. Despite her efforts to find affordable housing, she was directed to the camps located on the city's outskirts, where aid organizations provided intermittent assistance.

The outskirts of the city were a harrowing reminder of the atrocities of war. The displaced people, victims of the regime's bombings and attacks by their Russian and Iranian allies or battles led by the International Coalition to eliminate ISIS, fled to the seven official camps. However, they found no solace as the camps were already bursting at the seams, with over a quarter-million Syrians cramped into tiny tents made of worn-out blankets and sheets, some even made of tin. The tents were marked with the United Nations logo yet lacked basic necessities such as sanitation services and clean drinking water, which had to be brought in by tanker trucks. Medical services were in short supply, leaving women and children to wait for hours on end to receive treatment. In this dire situation, education was a luxury, and the only thing children could do was run around the camps and play in the dirt.

Sana quickly realized that the water was the most crucial issue. Women and children had to stand in line for hours to receive contaminated water, which led to numerous cases of diarrhea and cholera. It was a painful irony: they waited for water that caused health problems, and then they had to stand in line to receive medicine to overcome those same health issues. She couldn't find a place for herself in the overcrowded camps and decided to seek refuge in a makeshift camp.

# Chapter Twenty-Four
# Even the Sky Has No Mercy!

Sana finally found the refuge she needed. The small, worn-out tent she purchased from a family looking to leave the informal settlement was made of bags of aid sent by the United Nations. Inside, she had a small lamp without kerosene, a washing basin, a semi-empty box of washing powder, and a bucket for filling water. The land on which the tent was erected was sloping and rugged, surrounded by a number of semi-dry trees.

Despite these conditions, Sana was grateful to have a place she could call her own, free from the control of jailers, officers, security agents, warlords, or caliphs. She was in control over her own life again. Sana made friends in the camp and used her nursing skills to help anyone in need. In return, people gave her food and clothing.

Life in the camp was already challenging, especially in this particular camp that lacked anything reminiscent of life before the war. The world had abandoned these people. But for Sana, this was still easier compared to what she had experienced over the past years.

Then the rain came, pouring down like bullets, flooding the camp and turning the earth into mud. Personal belongings, clothes, dishes, and pots were swept away by torrents of water from inside the tents. Even an empty child's cradle was floating on the muddy water. Sana saw a little girl being dragged by the water, unable to move and submerged and floating in the torrent.

A woman quickly picked her up and held her upside down to let the water out of her mouth. An old woman hugged a tree trunk to avoid being swept away. Screams and crying filled the air.

The tents looked like boats moored on the seashore. More than fifty families stood amazed at the scene, having fled from bombing, persecution, killing, and torture, only to be faced with torrential rain. However, some tents on higher ground remained dry, and their owners received families whose tents were flooded. Sana's tent also survived, and she welcomed over ten people, including men, women, and children. They spent the evening chatting, some sleeping and some awake, and it felt like a scout camp.

Life in the camp was still challenging, but at this moment, they found solace in each other's company and the fact that they had survived the rain.

After the rain stopped the following morning, men, women, and children sprang into action, working together as one, each knowing what to do. They dug trenches between the tents to direct the water away, reinstalled the tents that had been pulled out of the ground, and used wooden pegs extracted from dry tree branches to secure the covers, blankets, and wet mattresses on trees in the sun. They collected belongings that had been washed away by the torrent and placed them in the middle of the camp for the owners to reclaim. They even built mud and stone fenders around the edges of the tents to brace for future waves of rain.

In the aftermath of the rain, life in the makeshift camp gradually returned to normal, and Sana's tent was soon emptied as everyone went back to their respective shelters. However, one elderly man with piercing eyes and disheveled hair remained in the corner of the tent, muttering incomprehensible words and dozing off intermittently. Sana discovered that he was from the

Hariri family in Daraa and had suffered unimaginable losses in recent years.

The man had once been known for his generosity and honesty, but his life had been shattered when his four children were arrested at the start of the demonstrations in the Omari Mosque. In less than a month, they were returned to him as lifeless bodies bearing marks of torture and mutilation. When he refused to sign a false statement claiming that they had died in a traffic accident, he was threatened with the rape and public humiliation of his wife and daughter. Unable to withstand the pressure, he ultimately signed the paper and buried his children alone with his grief.

Sana also encountered Mustafa, a man who had lost his wife and daughter in a bombing raid that had hit their home in Daraa al-Balad. Though he had survived the attack, Mustafa was plagued with grief and felt that he would rather have died with his loved ones. He now lived in a tent and relied on his neighbors for assistance with basic necessities like food and hygiene.

## Chapter Twenty-Five
## A Deformed Godot

Despite having lost everything, Mustafa held on to the hope of finding his daughter Wafa, who had been chosen by the Ministry of Education to work as a class teacher in eastern Ghouta. However, the siege imposed on Ghouta had cut off all communication with her, and he feared the worst. He longed to hear news of her, to know if she was still alive, but he was left with uncertainty and desperation.

In the midst of his grief, he found comfort in the company of Sana. As he sought refuge from the rain, he entered Sana's tent for the first time and was struck by the familiarity of her presence. She reminded him of his daughter, who was around the same age as Sana. Most of the time, he sat on the only chair in the tent, observing Sana's work as a nurse. She provided him with food and drink and offered him solace. Despite their limited conversations, he would sometimes accidentally call her Wafa, only to correct himself when he regained his composure.

As Mustafa continued to wait for news of his daughter, Sana remained a source of comfort and stability in his life.

*I have been waiting for Godot for what seems like years, just like Uncle Mustafa. We both wait for Godot to bring news about his daughter. We both cling to hope that comes from the depths of this harsh life. He wants the news to be good, and I want it to bring some kind of breakthrough. Deep down, we know that the result will not be what we hope for, but we still dream, dream that it will come.*

*Perhaps Godot will arrive in the form of a man of prestige and good looks, or a woman of grace and beauty, or a mixture between them. The important thing is that Godot brings hope, that he comes with the desired wishes. But there is also fear that he will come without a head, or without limbs, or that he will come with blindfolded eyes. The fear that he will come disfigured, mimicking our distorted life.*

Every evening, Sana and Mustafa would have tea together. Sana trusted him with the tragedies she endured and would divulge stories of her travels from Damascus to its countryside and onward to Hama, Raqqa, and finally Aleppo. She assumed he couldn't fathom her struggles, but regardless, she spoke in detail while he listened intently. His face, lined with wrinkles, often betrayed the weight of pain and sadness he carried, and on occasion, he would recite religious sayings like 'God protects us,' 'God is kind to us,' and 'There is no god but God over the oppressor.'

Their evening sessions extended for more than a month, with Sana relieving her pent-up emotions. Though she felt guilty for unloading on a man who had already undergone so much, her need to confide always won over her reservations. She persuaded herself that her hardships could help alleviate his own and that perhaps, knowing others like him suffered could assist in his recovery. If he didn't understand, she concluded, then their conversations wouldn't harm him.

He soaked in her words, experiencing every moment she recounted, grieving and celebrating with her, and feeling optimistic or despairing, depending on the progression of her story. He never made her feel like 'The Survivor,' a title that had become her alias in the camp. Rather, he kept her stories confidential, never disclosing them to anyone else. Whenever someone inquired about his whereabouts, he would respond with, "To see Sana." And if he encountered someone in need, he would lead them to her.

The moniker 'The Survivor' promptly circulated throughout the camp and surrounding areas, becoming familiar to everyone. Sana discovered that Uncle Mustafa was the one who coined the title, but instead of feeling bothered, she was proud.

# Chapter Twenty-Six
# The Talent of Criminality

The nickname 'The Survivor' had become synonymous with Sana in the camp and beyond, with even the local media taking notice of her story. One young journalist, convinced of the power of her message, approached Sana to be the focus of a video report that would be broadcast on social media. Eager to share her story of triumph in the face of adversity, Sana agreed. The report, titled 'The Survivor: Between the Regime and ISIS,' was produced by a well-known local network and included snapshots of Sana's life, a brief interview with the journalist, and some written sentences about her experiences.

The video quickly went viral on social media, reaching hundreds of thousands of viewers and generating an outpouring of sympathy. International media outlets took an interest in Sana's story. However, reaching her proved difficult, given her financial constraints and lack of a phone or social media presence.

Despite these challenges, an international channel eventually contacted Sana through intermediaries to conduct an interview with her. Thrilled at the opportunity to share her message with a wider audience, Sana was dismayed to learn that the channel only wanted to focus on her time in Raqqa under the rule of ISIS. Refusing to be pigeonholed, Sana insisted that the interview cover both the atrocities of the regime and ISIS and her experience with both. Eventually, the channel relented.

The interview lasted over two hours and was a grueling experience for Sana. At times, she cried and felt flashes of cold and heat across her body. Despite the hardship, Sana remained determined to remember and share every detail. Her words were sometimes spontaneous, at other times deliberate. The young broadcaster conducting the interview was lively and provocative, prodding Sana to share more. The interview revealed the full extent of Sana's tragedy and the atrocities she had faced. But despite the pain and hardship, Sana felt compelled to share all that she had gone through.

As the interview drew to a close, the young broadcaster asked Sana a final question, "Is there anything you would like to add?"

Sana took a moment to gather her thoughts before posing a question that had been weighing heavily on her mind, "What happened to me has happened to many of my countrymen, but what baffles me is where this talent for criminality comes from?" Her voice was filled with sadness and frustration, and her question lingered in the air long after the interview had ended.

A few days later, the interview was published under the title, *'Testimony of a Survivor: The Talent for Criminality between the Regime and ISIS.'* It quickly gained attention and brought Sana immense popularity in the region, with numerous media channels and websites requesting follow-up interviews. Sana declined them all, instead focusing on nursing and caring for her beloved Uncle Mustafa.

## Chapter Twenty-Seven
## Point of No Return

On that fateful evening, Sana was sitting with Uncle Mustafa in front of their tent, enjoying a cup of tea together. Their neighbor, Hamida, approached them with devastating news. One of her sons had arrived at the camp after a long journey, carrying with him another list of casualties from the bombing of the city of Douma. On that list was the name 'Wafaa,' Mustafa's daughter.

The news hit Mustafa hard, as he had lost all his hopes and remaining relatives. At first, he couldn't comprehend the situation and refused to believe it. He sat for hours in front of the tent, lost in contemplation, his pain palpable. Eventually, Mustafa attempted to stand up, seemingly wanting to go to his tent, but his steps betrayed him. He experienced violent contractions in his facial muscles until he lost consciousness completely.

Sana screamed for help, calling nearby tents to alert the Civil Defense. Within minutes, the Civil Defense arrived, and Sana administered first aid to Mustafa, making him comfortable with a pillow under his head and loosening his clothes. When the convulsions stopped, she carefully moved him to his side and prepared him for transportation. The Civil Defense team loaded Mustafa onto their vehicle after providing initial medical assistance, and Sana accompanied him to the hospital.

Minutes later, Sana found herself by Mustafa's side at the hospital, where he remained unconscious, hooked up to a breathing machine and a heart monitor. Doctors were busy analyzing his condition, speaking among themselves, but Mustafa was unable to communicate. Sana anxiously waited for the first light of dawn when one of the doctors approached her.

"Your father is in a very critical condition, and with our limited capabilities here, we are unable to provide the necessary treatment. We need to transfer him to Turkey," the doctor informed Sana, assuming Mustafa was her father and wanting to check if she understood the gravity of the situation.

"Do you know what happened to him?" Sana asked, her voice trembling with fear. The doctor placed a comforting hand on her shoulder, but his words offered little solace.

"The situation is very serious, and he may pass away at any moment. The attack he experienced has caused a defect in his heart, and we are uncertain if there is any damage to his brain."

As Sana stood there, contemplating whether to accompany Uncle Mustafa to Turkey or not, she felt torn. She had only managed to grab a small bag containing her money and some official papers before riding with the Civil Defense to the hospital. Despite not being Uncle Mustafa's daughter, she had helped him in the past, treating his injuries and assisting him when he needed help. However, only family members were usually allowed to accompany patients during transfers. Sana was aware that her own condition wouldn't permit her to go with Uncle Mustafa, but she also didn't want to leave him alone.

The ambulance team was waiting, ready to transport Uncle Mustafa. The team leader approached Sana with authority, taking her bag from her hand. Sana tried to explain that Uncle Mustafa was just her neighbor in the camp, not her father, and she had no identification papers. However, the team leader remained resolute.

"It doesn't matter if you're his daughter or not," he said

firmly. "What matters is that this man needs help. He needs a companion, someone to take care of him and assist him. And in emergency cases like this, identification papers are not checked."

He placed her bag inside the car and gestured for her to enter. Sana felt a sense of duty overwhelming her. She knew she had to help Uncle Mustafa. She walked toward the car. Little did she know that she was about to bid farewell to her homeland forever as she embarked on this trip with Uncle Mustafa to Turkey.

# Chapter Twenty-Eight
# Crucial Decisions

Sana spent over a month by Uncle Mustafa's bedside, talking to him, singing to him, and taking care of him. Despite his unconscious state, she had developed a close bond with him during this time. But now, the doctors had informed her that all attempts to help him had failed, and they needed her approval to turn off the medical devices that were keeping him alive. There had been no brain activity for more than ten days.

The doctor spoke to her in broken English, explaining that Uncle Mustafa's brain was no longer functioning, and he was no longer with them. As if that wasn't enough, the doctor also asked Sana if she would consider donating Uncle Mustafa's organs. A child in the intensive care unit needed a liver, and a woman needed a retina transplant to regain her sight. Uncle Mustafa's blood type matched theirs, and others could potentially benefit from his organs as well.

Sana tried to explain to the doctor that she was not related to Uncle Mustafa and had no authority to make medical decisions for him. She insisted that their connection was merely a coincidence and that she was not responsible for him. However, the doctor saw her as the one who had accompanied Uncle Mustafa and believed she had the authority to make these decisions.

Initially, Sana did not want to come with Uncle Mustafa in the first place. She had wanted to stay in her tent. But her instincts had led her to be by his side in the hospital. Now, she found herself in a position of controlling the destiny of a stranger. She had only known Uncle Mustafa for a few months, and their relationship had grown stronger during the days she had not left his room in the unfamiliar hospital. Sana did not want to be the one making these decisions, but the circumstances had put her in this position, and she had to make the right choices.

*After careful consideration, I have made a difficult decision. Unfortunately, my uncle Mustafa has passed away and is now in a state of brain death. He is essentially a body that cannot function without devices to make decisions on his behalf. Therefore, I have chosen to disconnect him from these devices, as it is the appropriate decision to make.*

Mustafa's family had a long history of sacrificing for their homeland, freedom, and dignity. Mustafa himself had followed in their footsteps, never holding back in his own sacrifices. It seemed only fitting to continue this tradition of generosity among other family members.

Sana informed the doctors of her decision to donate Uncle Mustafa's organs. She bid farewell to him by placing a loving kiss on his forehead before leaving him. The nurses stepped in, preparing Mustafa's body for the operating room, where his organs would be donated to save lives. As his bed was wheeled from the room to the corridor, hospital doctors and nurses lined both sides of the corridor, heads bowed in deep respect for Mustafa's selfless act. They touched his body with gratitude and love, acknowledging the lives he would help save through his organ donation.

Sana couldn't hold back her tears. Her tears were not only

for Uncle Mustafa but also for all her fellow countrymen who had perished in the past. She was deeply moved by the great respect that Mustafa, the last of them, was receiving from strangers, a respect that he did not always receive from his own people. The nurses outside the operating room consoled Sana, patting her shoulder and sitting beside her.

Hours later, the doctor emerged from the operating room with the news: "Mustafa helped save eight people today, including a child and three women," he said, placing his hand on Sana's shoulder. "The nurses are preparing him now; he will go to his final resting place."

After Uncle Mustafa's organs were donated to several families, they approached Sana, accompanied by the doctor, expressing their love and gratitude in words she couldn't understand but appreciated, nonetheless.

With the help of the hospital's doctors and nurses, in cooperation with the municipality of Gaziantep, the Turkish border city where they were located, Mustafa was buried. Sana insisted that he be buried in his shroud, wrapped in the flag of the revolution, as he had desired, in order to help others, and refused to have him washed[16].

The burial was attended by a small gathering of Syrians who had heard their story, as well as families of those who had received Mustafa's organs. They all read Al-Fatihah, a prayer for the deceased, and departed.

The municipality of Gaziantep provided Sana with refugee identification without any trouble and arranged for her to live in

---

[16] In the Islamic faith, a person who dies is usually washed, however, if a person is considered a martyr (shaheed), they are not to be washed. The reason the martyrs are not washed is because their blood would set them apart on the Day of Judgment.

a shared house in the city. They also sent her clothes, food, and other necessities that would last her for months. Despite offers from Turkish media to report on Uncle Mustafa and Sana's story, she declined, wanting to keep his sacrifice between him and his Creator. Nevertheless, some channels and newspapers spoke of a Syrian man who had given eight Turkish families extra years with their loved ones through his organ donation.

A new chapter in Sana's life has begun, one where she found herself in an unfamiliar city, speaking a language she didn't understand and once again feeling alone.

*Today marks the start of a new adventure in a city unknown to me, speaking a language I don't know. I have no choice but to move forward; returning to the tent is no longer an option. This city is filled with Syrians from all walks of life, and I can start afresh here. Perhaps it will be better than what I left behind.*

*For the first time in years, I am living a normal life. There is electricity, an uninterrupted water supply, a working TV, a refrigerator with cold water, markets, cars, and people walking the neighborhoods and streets without fear. I am overwhelmed with amazement. Though I used to live like this years ago in Damascus, the long separation from civilization makes it feel like a brand-new experience. No planes bombing, no deafening cannons, no destruction, no field hospitals, no death, no blood, no restrictions, no imposed dress code, no chains controlling my life or men in suits controlling my thoughts.*

# Chapter Twenty-Nine
# Obsessions

The past years had made Sana capable of adjusting to any circumstance, and the current situation was better than ever. However, the past shocks she experienced since 2011 and the conditions she endured during those years were the real challenge. Coping with difficult circumstances was something she had mastered, whereas coping with easy, mundane circumstances felt difficult now!

She could do whatever she wanted, wear whatever she wanted, live as she pleased, speak freely, express her opinions without fear of eavesdroppers, and rebel against her reality if she desired. All this freedom felt burdensome. She used to live under guardianship and manage within those constraints, but now she no longer needed to deceive or find ways to survive. She could truly live now.

Like other southern Turkish provinces, Gaziantep served as a destination for Syrian refugees fleeing the horrors of war, seeking a chance at life and escaping death. Some relied on aid provided by the Turkish government in camps, while others ventured on their own to integrate into the social and economic fabric of the country. Many of them succeeded in adapting to the cities they arrived in and became an integral part of their communities.

Sana was no exception. Within the first few months of her arrival in the city, she found a job as an English teacher in a school. She immersed herself in daily life, searching for a sense of purpose. Although she had managed to suppress her trauma in Syria, the defense mechanisms she resorted to during times of danger were no longer effective. Her mind was still trapped in Syria, reliving memories of detention, torture, and bombardment, with images of corpses and severed limbs haunting her in nightmares.

Despite forming a small community of friends and achieving financial stability, she struggled to fully integrate. She tried various methods, such as meditation and relaxation exercises, she found online, to confront her fears and quiet her mind, but to no avail. Details of past incidents grew clearer in her mind instead of fading away as if they were multiplying and reproducing. They persisted, entwined in every single part of her brain.

# Chapter Thirty
# Bread Is Cheap, and Human Life Is Expensive

Sana spent a year in Turkey, immersing herself in the language, forming friendships, and building a small community. Although she found a sense of safety and freedom in the city, her unwavering determination was solely focused on escaping to Europe, joining the thousands of Syrians, Afghans, Iraqis, and Iranians in a mass migration that had been ongoing for years. She yearned to begin anew in a land far removed from the darkness of war, destruction, bombing, torture, and death that she had endured. Despite warnings about the dangers of sea voyages and news of sinking boats and refugee deaths, her determination remained unwavering. She believed that moving to the farthest corners of the earth held the solution.

*Being as far away as possible is the solution. I have to go as far away from my country as possible. I need to find solace in a new homeland where human life is valued more than anything. I will go wherever I can, and nothing will stop me. Perhaps there, I will find the peace I seek, and maybe I will find Godot, whom I have been waiting for, hoping that he will help me conquer the haunting memories and finally enjoy a restful night's sleep, free from nightmares and disturbing dreams.*

Sana made thorough preparations for her trip and managed to

save a total of 4000 dollars during her year-long stay in Turkey. Smugglers seemed to be everywhere. However, the real challenge was in selecting the best and most reliable smuggler, which was easier said than done. The primary concern was finding the most suitable price, considering that smugglers charged anywhere between one thousand and ten thousand dollars, depending on the chosen method and level of comfort.

Sana consulted her friends and inquired about prices and various routes. She met several smugglers in dubious cafes and sought information from individuals who had successfully reached Europe. Some had opted for sea routes to Greece or Italy, followed by train journeys, while others crossed the river between Turkey and Greece on foot. There were also those who departed directly from Turkish airports, heading straight to their final destinations in Germany or Sweden.

In Gaziantep, there was a renowned smuggler known as Al-Tunisi, who had gained fame for facilitating the journey of numerous Syrians and people of other nationalities to Europe. The clandestine nature of their meeting was crucial, considering the constant pursuit of smugglers by local authorities, resulting in their imprisonment. Sana introduced herself and took a seat, eager to hear what Al-Tunisi had to say.

Al-Tunisi began his speech calmly and composed, immediately reassuring Sana that he was a seasoned professional.

"Let's get straight to the point," Al-Tunisi began. "You have several options, the first being air travel. With a Syrian passport, you can depart from any airport in Turkey to an African country, typically Cameroon or the Congo. There, you will meet a trusted security officer who will facilitate your journey. After a day's stay, you will proceed with a European passport, most likely Italian. From there, you can take a flight to Sweden. This route will cost you between ten thousand and twelve thousand euros, but it guarantees a hundred percent safe passage."

Curious about alternative routes, Sana inquired, "What about other options?"

"We have a route that involves crossing the Marsiche River from the Turkish city of Edirne. This journey requires significant walking, starting from Edirne and continuing until you reach the riverbank. A small boat awaits to transport the group in batches to the Greek side. From there, you'll embark on a walk toward the edge of the international highway. At that point, you'll be met by several cars that will take you to the nearest city. From there, each person can choose their desired route," Al-Tunisi explained.

Curious about the reliability of this method and the course of action upon reaching Athens, Sana asked, "Is this method guaranteed? And what will I do after reaching Athens, for example?"

"This method relies on trial and error. If the group gets arrested, the Turkish authorities typically detain them in a detention center for a day before releasing them. Then, we make another attempt. The cost of this trip is 2000 USD," Al-Tunisi clarified. "As for your second question, you can either rely on luck or we can provide you with a fake Spanish residency, enabling you to book a flight to your desired destination. With a closer resemblance to Westerners, you'll be less likely to arouse suspicion."

The option of traveling by plane was not feasible for Sana, and the river route did not convince her, as evidenced by her expression. This prompted al-Tunisi to propose a third option.

"Of course, you have the most common option: traveling by sea to Greece or Italy. In this case, we specifically offer the route to Greece. You have several choices available. You can opt for rubber boats, which are very dangerous but relatively inexpensive, usually costing between five hundred and eight hundred dollars. Alternatively, there's the option of a larger boat. The prices for this range between 1500 USD and 5000 USD. I have a three-class boat scheduled to depart in a few days. The first-class costs 5000, the second class is 2,500, and the third class is 1500," Al-Tunisi presented the available options.

Sana's decision became clear. The amount of money she possessed would determine the type of journey she could undertake. She opted not to settle for the third-class option but instead chose to ride in the second-class section of the boat, which cost 2500 USD. This left her with an additional two thousand five hundred dollars to cover her travel from Greece to Sweden.

# Chapter Thirty-One
# Crossing the Sea on a Fragile Boat

After the long years Sana spent on land, she found herself facing the vast, unpredictable sea. The boat she boarded was in a dilapidated state, with rust covering its sides. Its original gray color was barely visible, only appearing in small patches. The boat consisted of three levels: the engine room, the middle deck, and the deck. Standing on the beach, Sana joined over two hundred people, all eagerly waiting to board the boat. However, it was clear that the boat could only accommodate a maximum of a hundred people. Among the crowd were children, women, and individuals of various ages and nationalities. Most were Syrians, but there were also Afghans, Africans, and Iranians, all filled with anticipation.

Everyone was instructed not to bring any belongings except for what could fit in a small bag. The rest of their possessions were discarded on the beach. Most of the Africans and Afghans were assigned to the engine room, while the remaining passengers were divided between the middle deck and the main deck. The smugglers or boat operators did not board the vessel themselves. Interestingly, the Captain turned out to be one of the refugees who had prior experience in boat navigation. Sana later learned that he traveled for free in exchange for his agreement with the Tunisian smuggler to sail the boat.

Sana made a rough estimation, considering the payment made by a hundred people ranging from 1500–5000 USD. It became apparent that the smugglers had acquired the boat for no less than 250,000 dollars. The smugglers exploited desperate individuals who were left with no choice but to rely on them for their journey. These people were filled with hope for a better future, a country that would respect their rights and provide them with a decent life, far from dictatorships, extremist organizations, and armed groups.

With apprehension in the air, the journey began. The passengers exchanged glances, their fear and anxiety evident. A woman in her thirties clung tightly to her two children and began to pray. A young man in his twenties sat silently in a corner, his face tense yet filled with hope. Meanwhile, a man in his forties sold all his belongings to embark on this journey, leaving his young children with his wife, hoping to reach a new country and reunite with his family. Before embarking, he had left his will, instructing his children to obey their mother in the event of his death.

As the passengers prepared to embark on their journey, numerous instructions were given to ensure their safety. They were advised to remain seated and not to walk around the boat. Sana couldn't help but wonder how anyone could even move in such a crowded vessel. The trip was expected to take two to two and a half hours, ultimately reaching the Greek island of Lesbos, leaving each person to fend for themselves from there onward.

The initial half-hour of the journey seemed relatively calm. Everyone was seated, barely any movement was detected, and conversations were held in hushed tones. Even the children appeared remarkably composed, either whispering or peacefully asleep. The faces around Sana seemed to oscillate between dreaminess and gloominess. However, she knew that despite the varying emotions, everyone aboard shared a common thread:

they saw this journey, this fragile boat, as their lifeline. Each person held their own dreams, but they all converged in this vessel, united in the hope of finding the 'Godot' they sought in their destination—a place of refuge. Children, women, young adults, and the elderly—all of them waited, still trapped in the spiral of survival, yearning to prevail over the sea, seeking asylum, and striving to overcome the perils of politics and war so they could shape their own destiny and truly live.

## Chapter Thirty-Two
## At Sea

The rest of the voyage, however, proved to be far from the ease experienced during the first half-hour. The wind picked up, causing the boat to sway and the bow to collide with the waves. Attempts to stand up only intensified the boat's motion, creating a sense of imminent capsizing. Cries and mournful wails filled the air as women and children huddled together along the sides of the vessel. Men wept, prayers grew louder, and the captain shouted from the cockpit, desperately urging everyone to remain still. The engine roared, its strained sounds reminiscent of grinding rusty iron.

Fear was palpable, including within Sana, who sat cross-legged, silent, her face etched with horror. Had the hour of their demise arrived? To perish in a boat at sea! The media didn't dub these vessels 'death boats' for nothing.

The storage hold, also known as the engine hold or the third level, as referred to by al-Tunisi, was the site of a series of rapidly unfolding events. Tragically, the emissions from the engine claimed the lives of three young Africans who were in close proximity, leading to their suffocation. Their bodies remained untouched, as nobody dared to disturb them or make any movement that could jeopardize the safety of the boat and its passengers.

Two hours into the voyage, the engine failed, causing the boat to come to a halt in the open sea. The once turbulent waves began to calm, and the winds gradually lost their strength, leading to a period of tranquil surrender.

In a state of urgency, the captain cried out, "Is there anyone on board who can repair the engine?"

A man in his fifties, with shaggy hair and a dark complexion, stood up and declared, "I am a mechanic." He accompanied the captain down to the engine room, where they were joined by several other men. They dropped anchor to avoid being swayed by the waves and commenced their repair work, determined to fix the engine and resume their journey.

As the wind subsided and the waves diminished, a sense of movement returned to the boat. Women tended to the needs of the children, while the men engaged in discussions, searching for potential solutions. The bodies of the three deceased young African men were carefully brought to the surface, their bodies wrapped in makeshift blankets. Placed at the front of the boat, a group of men organized themselves and offered a hasty funeral prayer. Sana assisted in the process, helping to wrap the deceased in blankets and wiping their faces, which were stained by the emissions from the engine.

After concluding their prayer, the men solemnly carried the three bodies and recited verses from the Koran before casting them into the sea. The boat couldn't accommodate them any longer.

Several hours passed, and the engine still refused to start. Everyone waited anxiously as the men worked in the storage hold. The sun had set, and they were faced with spending the night at sea.

# Chapter Thirty-Three
# Summer Storm

All movement on the boat ceased. Repair attempts proved futile. People scattered and found solace in their own corners, surrounded by family and friends. The voices gradually faded, turning into whispers and eventually complete silence. It seemed as if they were asleep, but the truth was that despair had gripped the hearts of most aboard. The boat did not sleep that night. Each person remained lost in their own thoughts, awaiting deliverance.

Sana contemplated their situation, likening it to waiting for Godot. Everyone was waiting, yearning for a miracle or any sign of relief from their predicament—a dilapidated boat, a non-functional engine, an overwhelming number of passengers, corpses, children, women, men, and the elderly. They all waited for Godot, but instead, they were met with a fierce storm.

As the sun rose, the sea roared once again. The boat was tossed left and right by the violent waves, and everyone clung to their positions, desperately trying to remain on the deck. The air was filled with screams and cries piercing through the sky as women and children expressed their fear. Men, too, felt the weight of their anxiety, striving to maintain composure.

A woman held her five-year-old son tightly with her hands, gripping a small pole near the cockpit with her feet. Tears streamed down her cheeks as she whispered, "Oh, my dear... oh, my dear..." Sana, like everyone else, clung to the side of the boat, clutching one of the poles with all her might.

An elderly man lay on the ground, struggling to hold onto anything. With each crashing wave, his body teetered dangerously close to falling off the boat. Fortunately, another man extended a helping hand, pulling him to safety and securing his grip on the side of the boat.

A family consisting of a man, a woman, and three children between the ages of twelve and sixteen huddled together, embracing one another. The woman held a bag, seemingly containing all their belongings, with the father and the three youngsters surrounding her, holding on tightly.

Despite ongoing attempts to repair the engine, it seemed increasingly impossible, especially with the relentless rain and the fury of the waves. Even though it was summer, their anxiety heightened with each passing moment.

The anchor was lifted from the depths of the sea, and the boat began to move, weighed down by the presence of its passengers and the heavy rain. Progress was sluggish, providing a temporary sense of safety. However, the wind had a different plan. It violently swept a man off the deck, and despite efforts to save him, he was lost to the depths. Meanwhile, the woman who clung to her child and the pole lost her grip. She found herself on one side while her child remained on the other. A pole, shattered by the strength of the wind, fell upon her, and within moments, she took her last breath.

Her child was left alone, crying and reaching out to his deceased mother, but the wind tossed him in all directions. He approached Sana, who clung to the iron of the boat. Sana grabbed him, embracing him tightly against her chest, and wept alongside him.

# Chapter Thirty-Four
# On Top of Death the Grave Tightens[17]

The dilapidated boat began to crack, the iron creaked, and the wood exploded beneath their feet. Water flooded the boat from all sides, accompanied by cries, screams, and desperate pleas. Minds froze in fear and panic. An elderly man lost his sanity and started jumping erratically while a woman sang at the top of her lungs. Another woman, overcome by despair, removed her clothes and leaped into the water. At the front of the boat, a man shouted with all his might, "Lord, save us!" In a desperate act, another man threw his children into the sea before plunging after them.

    Chaos, noise, tension, and commotion engulfed the boat's deck, blending with the crashes and screams emanating from the sea. Amidst it all, Sana remained calm. Suddenly, she exclaimed, "I refuse to die here." And took action. Clutching the child, she made her way to the starboard side of the boat, where she had noticed a rope earlier. She grabbed hold of the rope and, using her foot, broke off a plank from the boat's deck. Hurling it into the sea, she jumped in after it, placing the child safely on the plank. Securing the plank to her body with the rope, she began swimming.

    Passengers jumped in after her, but she eluded them, determined to swim away from the doomed boat. The waves

---

[17] Famous Syrian proverb to indicate that a situation has gone from bad to worse

pushed her back toward the boat, prompting her to forcefully strike the water and create distance once more.

It didn't take long for the boat to sink beneath the waves, no more than ten minutes. Some of the passengers who knew how to swim fought against the relentless waves, while those who couldn't sink to the depths with the vessel.

Finally, the storm subsided. Those who were able to continue to paddle, using whatever piece of wood or debris they could find, while those who couldn't sink into the same fate as those who went before them. The boat, originally carrying over two hundred people, vanished, leaving only around fifty survivors. Bodies, mostly of women and children, began to float to the surface one by one.

Hours passed as the remaining passengers drifted aimlessly at sea, resigned to their impending fate. But Sana refused to succumb to despair. She had endured worse, and she would not give up.

She pressed on, swimming against the frigid water, currents, and scorching sun. Hours beget hours, but she persevered, swimming with unwavering determination. Her hands and feet grew numb, yet she continued to strike the water and kick with all her might, alternating between her back and chest. The strength she summoned was extraordinary.

Initially, the child cried while on the plank tied to Sana's body, but gradually, the cries ceased, replaced by silence. She could no longer hear him, but she couldn't afford to divert her attention. She swam on until she caught sight of a beach in the distance. Uncertain if she had returned to Turkey or reached Greece, she paid little mind. All that mattered was reaching land or at least coming close.

A small fishing boat approached, catching her eye. She

attempted to cry out for help, but her voice failed her. Exhaustion from swimming had depleted her energy.

*In those peculiar moments, I found myself in an eerie state. Though I was still breathing, I felt lifeless, as if I were already dead. My organs floated within the water, yet my senses slipped away. The scorching sun mercilessly burned my cheeks while the icy water seemed to freeze the very blood in my veins. My skin took on a pallid, ghostly hue with sporadic veins of pink. Amidst it all, a single phrase reverberated relentlessly in my mind: 'Don't give up, don't give up, don't give up…'*

# Chapter Thirty-Five
# When Her Own Voice Failed Her

Sana's journey through perilous waters was a harrowing experience that tested her courage. As she struggled to call for help, her voice failed her, leaving her helpless in the vast expanse of the sea. Yet, her determination remained undeterred as her limbs tirelessly propelled her toward the distant boat, hoping for salvation.

Questions raced through her mind—would they notice her? Would they rescue her? With every stroke through the water, the fear of imminent death slowly retreated. Hope for survival flickered within her.

Eventually, the boat drew closer, and Sana and the child she had protected were pulled to safety. However, her voice remained silenced. Exhausted, she lay on the boat's roof, covered in aluminum sheets. Her mind refused to succumb to sleep; she yearned to check on the child. But her body, paralyzed by fatigue, prevented her from moving.

With only her eyes capable of movement, Sana scanned the boat's deck, searching for the child. She spotted him approaching, wrapped in aluminum and smiling. Overwhelmed with relief, he nestled into her embrace, finding solace in her presence. Although she couldn't physically reciprocate the hug, the safety she provided brought him comfort. Soon, they both drifted into a peaceful slumber.

Hours later, Sana awoke on the beach, surrounded by the

boat's crew in Greece. Her immediate happiness faded as she remembered those left behind. The crew informed her that the Turkish Coast Guard had rescued the remaining survivors adrift at sea, returning them to Turkey.

Their journey, marked by desperation and separation, epitomized the harsh realities faced by countless others seeking refuge across treacherous waters.

# Chapter Thirty-Six
# Mama Sana

The sea spat Sana and the young boy onto the shores of the Greek island of Lesbos, pushing them together onto this new land. Drenched, exhausted, and bereft of help, Sana was now unexpectedly responsible for the life of a child, a child who had lost his mother and sought refuge in her care. With barely a handful of dollars hidden in her chest and her identity papers lost in the storm, the future seemed grim.

"Mama Sana, what now?" The boy finally spoke, his small voice breaking the silence.

Surprised by his address, Sana paused. Wondering how the boy knew her name, she realized the more pressing question was why he called her 'mama.'

Seated on the sand, at eye level with the little boy, she managed a soft smile. "What's your name?"

"My name is Mayar," he replied.

"Mayar means the face of goodness and hope," Sana explained, trying to bring a touch of positivity.

She didn't need to ask why he called her 'mama.' He had chosen her to fill the void left by his mother, whom he had seen drown.

Their immediate need was to reach Athens, but their bedraggled appearance may draw unwanted attention. Sana had to secure new clothes and a means of communication. With her meager stash of dollars, she bought only the essentials, resolved to make every penny count.

Taking to the streets, they attempted to hitch a ride but faced rejection after rejection. Finally, a transport vehicle stopped. The driver, empathetic to their plight, agreed to take them closer to the capital.

Hiding among goods in the truck, they embarked on a grueling journey. Crossing ferries from Lesbos to Cesme, then to Lavrio, they rode through rough seas for twenty hours, finally reaching a highway close to Athens.

# Chapter Thirty-Seven
# Without Documents

As the sun ascended, they reached Athens. Passing by Victoria Park, the driver explained its colloquial name as 'Afghan Park,' witnessing migrants bedding down under the open sky, turning a public space into a makeshift haven.

Sana thanked the driver profusely and secured his contact details, intending to update him later. Setting foot in Omonia Square, a bustling hub notorious for smugglers in an even busier commercial district, they were surrounded by a mosaic of cultures—shops run by Asians and multilingual signs in English, Hindi, Arabic, and Greek.

Stunned by the Middle Eastern feel within Europe, they stumbled upon a humble eatery bearing the word 'Falafel' in Arabic. Ordering two sandwiches, Sana attempted to pay with dollars, only to be kindly refused; the workers, in a moment of solidarity, exchanged her dollars for euros and insisted on covering the bill.

Seated by the roadside, a dialogue in Arabic caught Sana's attention—two men discussing plans to reach Sweden or Germany. Intrigued, she approached them, sharing her own plight. They directed her to a smuggler's café, assuring her that they'd approach her there.

Hours elapsed in the café, but no one approached them. Doubt flickered in Sana's mind. An account sheet arrived with a cryptic note: 'Be at the café at eight in the evening, bring your documents.' She wandered the streets, witnessing impoverished families, and shuddered at the thought of sharing their fate.

Night fell, and she returned to the designated café, Mayar nestled on her lap. A young Pakistani approached, fluent in Arabic:

"Where are you headed, and what documents do you have?" he inquired.

"To Sweden, I don't have any documents on me; they were lost at sea," Sana confessed, putting forward their predicament.

# Chapter Thirty-Eight
# Between Land and Air

The Pakistani smuggler was sitting in a modest coffee shop in a dark corner. Sana thought he resembled a crow. He offered her detailed explanations:

"We can arrange air travel for you. We provide fake passports and European residence permits. You deposit the fees at an office, and upon arrival, we retrieve the payment. If you get caught, no need to pay; we'll handle the loss," he explained. "It costs fifteen hundred euros per travel document."

Sana, adding in Mayar's expenses, realized she didn't have enough money.

"And traveling by land?" she inquired.

"It's a strenuous journey for a child. Many hours of walking," he cautioned. Despite this, Sana could endure the trek.

"Previously, we used main crossings, but now, with increased patrols, we use side routes," he added. "The trip takes five to seven days and involves daily walks for over ten hours, using trains, cars, and buses. The land journey costs five hundred euros per person for the smuggler, plus about two hundred euros for each transportation link."

She explained her limited funds—only 2,300 USD—and Mayar's challenges with the land trip, pleading for assistance. Promising to consider her situation, the Pakistani said he would answer her in the morning.

Sana and Mayar spent the night outdoors, seeking refuge in

a secluded garden. Embracing Mayar, Sana collapsed on the grass, fatigue overwhelming her.

The following morning, at the café, the smuggler finally arrived, proposing a solution that could work.

"We deposit the funds, provide documents, and if arrested, you bear half the loss. If you succeed, someone will wait for you at the airport in Sweden to reclaim the documents for reuse. The departure in two days," he offered.

Sana had no other choice but to agree to his plan.

# Chapter Thirty-Nine
# Syrian-Spanish

For forty-eight hours, Sana did nothing but wait in the park near the café. Taking care of Mayar and reminiscing about her past consumed her time. Each reflection seemed to amplify the details of her experiences, making her relive the events.

On the third day, a young man, previously seen serving at the café, approached and handed her a small note. It read: 'Tonight, at eight, in the café. Don't be late.'

She arrived an hour early, taking her usual seat. The clock ticked by. Eight turned to nine, yet there was no sign of the person she expected. An anxious air enveloped her as Mayar dozed off on her chest. Questions besieged her mind, leaving her anxious and unwilling to leave the café.

At eleven, the Pakistani man finally entered.

"The papers are ready for you and the child," he said.

Sana was relieved as she inquired about their next step.

He handed her an envelope containing Spanish residencies and a flight reservation from Athens to Stockholm the next morning at six.

"We have not changed your nationality; this will make things easier. Stick to your Syrian identity; it's the truth and simplifies matters," he advised.

Emphasizing the importance of Mayar's silence in preserving the plan, he ensured they matched their story, provided a colorful bag, changed their attire, and drove them to the airport. Dropping them off at the entrance, he bid farewell.

*This is it. I am so close. I will make it. My story can't end here. I will reach my destination,* Sana reassured herself, determined to forge ahead.

# Chapter Forty
# At the Airport

Sana summoned all of her strength as she walked toward the airport entrance. Mayar clung to her white dress, his eyes drifting in and out of drowsiness. *This is the final moment, the last chapter,* she thought to herself, steeling herself for what lay ahead.

She mustered a smile and walked on, hiding her inner turmoil behind a facade of relief.

Approaching the ticket counter, she handed over the Spanish IDs with a single word 'Stockholm.' The employee glanced at her, and she diverted attention by caressing Mayar's hair and planting a kiss on his forehead. The employee handed her the boarding passes and signaled for her to place her bag on the scale. The weight seemed insignificant, but she remained unfazed. After tagging the bag, the employee handed her the second part of the label.

One hurdle cleared, and she headed toward the exit officer. Standing in line, she anticipated no passport stamp due to her European residency. However, she still needed clearance from the officer.

She felt the entire queue could hear her heart pounding. Anxiety and tension engulfed her. As the line slowly progressed, Mayar grew weary. She lifted him, cradling him around her neck, and he fell asleep instantly.

As she approached the officer, she placed her travel

documents and phone on the table. The officer examined the papers closely, and Sana offered a smile, turning slightly to display the sleeping child. A reassuring smile from the officer eased her fears momentarily. It was a bittersweet feeling.

Gesturing her to proceed, the officer's approval brought a sigh of relief. She kissed Mayar, thankful to pass smoothly. Moving only a few steps, she was startled by the officer's call, "Madame!" Panic surged within her, fearing she had been discovered and would be arrested. Her heart raced, sweat beading on her brow. She pretended not to hear, continuing forward.

Suddenly, a hand touched her back, turning her around. Fear gripped her until she saw the officer smiling. "You forgot your phone," he said.

With a faint smile and a quiet thank you, she took her phone and hurried on, relief flooding through her despite the initial scare.

## Chapter Forty-One
## The Heart's Roar

As the plane's engines roared and the flight attendant began the safety instructions through the loudspeaker, Sana felt a mix of anticipation and apprehension. The familiar request to fasten seat belts appeared on the screen, signaling the plane's departure.

With just four hours separating her from her final destination, Sana attempted to rest. Ironically, sleep eluded her despite any proper rest over the last few days. Meanwhile, Mayar slept soundly, his eyelids closing as he slipped into a peaceful slumber, his hand finding solace in Sana's grasp.

Those four hours seemed to stretch endlessly as thoughts raced through her mind. Should she turn herself in at the airport and seek asylum? What if they refused and sent her back to Athens? Maybe it was better to enter the country and then seek asylum, but she knew no one there, didn't understand the language, and had no clue about the new land. What would she do with Mayar? She would adopt him. But what if they accused her of child smuggling?

An internal dialogue persisted throughout the journey, a cascade of conflicting thoughts—what-ifs, hows, and whys.

"Fasten your seatbelts," the captain's voice interrupted her thoughts. "We are preparing to land in Stockholm."

Sana snapped back, summoning the composed demeanor she had rehearsed in her mind. She devised a narrative—a woman visiting relatives and friends with her son. But who were these relatives? What if someone asked for specifics? Sana tried to fabricate an entire scenario, creating names and residences in her head.

*This is the culmination of my journey. I have finally arrived,* she thought, drawing strength from within. *This is where my new life begins, with my new child, free from authoritarianism, fear, dependency, terror, and all that I have left behind.*

# Chapter Forty-Two
# The Meeting

She grasped Mayar's hand firmly and hastened toward the airport exit, forgetting everything else in her urgency—the bag, the person awaiting the ID cards, her well-rehearsed plans, and the composed façade she had prepared. Her pace was more akin to a hurried run, feeling as though her heart might leap out of her chest, its frantic beats resonating in her ears and seemingly reaching everyone around, yet propelling her forward.

Surprisingly, no one stopped her.

As she entered the main hall, her heart rate gradually slowed. She looked around at the bustling crowd—dozens, even hundreds of people moving in every direction, chatting, laughing, embracing, and dragging luggage behind them. Her bag, the man awaiting the papers—they crossed her mind fleetingly, but their significance had faded. What mattered now was that they had made it, and those contents held no value at this moment.

Standing amidst the airport's commotion, holding Mayar's hand, she felt a gentle tap on her shoulder.

"Welcome."

The voice spoke Arabic behind her, freezing her in place. She didn't turn.

The voice persisted, "Sana, how are you?"

Familiar yet unrecognizable. She turned.

"Mansour!"

She couldn't believe her eyes. Was he truly Mansour after all these years? How did he know she was arriving, and what brought him to Sweden? What should she say?

But he beat her to it.

"I recognized you from your white dress and your walk," Mansour said, smiling. "It's like the dress I first saw you in."

Sana was still in shock as Mansour stood there, allowing her to process this unforeseen reunion. Minutes passed in silence; her stunned gaze met by his smiling face.

Then, overcome with emotion, she rushed into his embrace, tears streaming down her face. Mayar joined in crying, and Mansour, too, couldn't contain his emotions.

Kisses, tears, and hugs followed.

She held him close, caressed his face, and took a step back as if confirming, "Is this real?" She needed assurance she wasn't dreaming.

"Am I dreaming?" she asked, choked with emotions.

Mansour smiled, replying, "Of course not. I'm here to meet a friend. Just as destiny brought us together years ago, it brings us together today."

Tears continued to flow, hugs ensued, and conversations poured out.

That day marked the conclusion of her journey.

*I've waited for Godot for so long, not realizing he was destiny. I mistook him for the savior, the hero, the leader—so many possibilities. Yet, he embodies destiny. Despite not showing me much mercy all these years, he's finally changed everything.*

Mansour offered invaluable help with procedures, papers, and logistics.

They conversed for hours, Sana sharing her detailed story of what she'd endured. Mansour revealed he'd been searching for her for years, having spotted her in a television program. He'd attempted to reach out but failed.

He proposed that she collaborate with a human rights group to prosecute war criminals. They agreed to testify at the International Criminal Court together.

## Chapter Forty-Three
## And the Story Unfolds

Entering a hall bustling with judges, lawyers, and journalists, Sana's presence drew significant attention owing to the news of her testimony and the scattered excerpts detailing her experiences.

Standing at the podium, Mayar by her side, she began her speech:

"It was in the early days of March, 2011, when I received an invitation to see a play adapted from Samuel Beckett's epic play, *Waiting for Godot*. It was there that I first met Mansour," gesturing toward him. It was then that everything began.

# Previously Published by Author

*Films Under the Microscope* (Study), 2024, Noon 4 Publishing.
*A Scarf and a Heavy Stick* (Diary), 2024, Khutwa Publishing.